Snowflakes in September

Stories about God's Mysterious Ways

Corrie Ten Boom
Elizabeth Sherrill
& others

DIMENSIONS

FOR LIVING

NASHVILLE

SNOWFLAKES IN SEPTEMBER

First Dimensions for Living edition 1992

Copyright © 1991 by Guideposts Associates, Inc., Carmel, NY 10512

Second Printing 1992

This book is printed on recycled, acid-free paper.

Library of Congress Cataloging-in-Publication Data

Snowflakes in September : stories about God's mysterious ways / Corrie Ten Boom . . . [et al.] — 1st Dimensions for Living ed.
    p. cm.
    Stories and poems originally published in Guideposts magazine from 1956 to 1989.
    ISBN 0-68738782-5 (alk. paper)
    1. Providence and government of God. I. Ten Boom, Corrie.
BT96.2.S58   1992
231.7—dc20   91-42389
                                                                                  CIP

All Scripture quotations, unless otherwise noted, are from the King James or Authorized Version of the Bible.

Scripture quotations marked RSV are from the Revised Standard Version of the Bible, copyright 1946, 1952, 1971 by the Division of Christian Education of the National Council of the Churches of Christ in the United States of America and are used by permission.

Scripture quotations marked NIV are from the New International Version of the Bible, copyright © 1978 by New York International Bible Society, and are used by permission.

Scripture quotations marked TLB are from *The Living Bible*, copyright 1971 owned by transfer to Illinois Marine Bank N.A. (as trustee). Used by permission of Tyndale House Publisher, Wheaton, IL 60188.

Scripture quotations marked NEB are from *The New English Bible*, copyright © 1976 by the Delegates of the Oxford University Press and the Syndics of the Cambridge University Press and are used by permission.

Every attempt has been made to credit the sources of copyrighted material used in this book. If any such acknowledgment has been inadvertently omitted or miscredited, receipt of such information would be appreciated.

Except as noted below, and for some poems, all material is reprinted from *Guideposts* magazine. Copyright © 1956, 1961, 1966, 1972, 1974, 1976, 1980, 1981, 1982, 1983, 1984, 1985, 1986, 1987, 1988, 1989 by Guideposts Associates, Inc., Carmel, NY 10512.

"The Crown of Thorns" by Caryll Houselander was adapted from *Caryll Houselander, That Divine Eccentric*, by Maisie Ward. Reprinted with permission of Sheed & Ward, Kansas City, MO.

MANUFACTURED IN THE UNITED STATES OF AMERICA

Snowflakes
in
September

Contents

Preface

Elizabeth Sherrill flew to New Mexico for a one-day seminar, and the airline lost her bag containing her one good pair of shoes. "What a time for this to happen!" she thought. She wouldn't know until the close of the conference that those missing shoes would literally save her life.

Kathy and her husband were waiting to adopt a baby. Early one July morning Kathy was startled awake by a vivid dream about a baby. What a happy dream! Surely they'd have their baby soon. How surprised she would be several months later to discover the significance of the date of her dream.

One September Doris Hartvig felt a great urge to crochet snowflakes. She couldn't explain her urge, but she bought an instruction book anyway and went to work on the snowflakes. Little did she know that several months later her snowflakes would make someone's dream of a very special Christmas tree come true.

Many of us have experienced "snowflakes in September"— ordinary and extraordinary moments when God's mysterious ways impact our lives and reassure us that we are not subject to mere chance but are part of a divine design. These moments offer dramatic proof of God's active and personal love for us.

This is a collection of "snowflakes in September." These true stories about God's mysterious ways are told by persons who have experienced firsthand God's active presence in their lives. These awe-inspiring accounts of God's transforming power and constant love call us to a renewed and wonder-filled faith.

God moves in ways we cannot always understand. May the wonder and joy of God's mystery enable you to recognize and celebrate the "snowflakes in September."

Snowflakes
in
September

GOD
Directs
OUR PATHS

Trust in the Lord with all thine heart. . . . In all thy ways acknowledge him, and he shall direct thy paths.

—PROVERBS 3:5–6

GOD'S PLANS
—Author Unknown

He will silently plan for thee;
His purposes shall all unfold.
The tangled skein shall shine at last,
A masterpiece of skill untold.

He will silently plan for thee,
Happy child of a Father's care,
As though no other claimed His love,
But thou alone to Him wert dear.

 ## THE SECURITY GUARD
Dorothy Nicholas

We were sitting at the table in our Florida home and talking to our next-door neighbors. This young couple had helped us a lot in the past year and a half, after my stroke and my husband's leg injury.

Unexpectedly, the husband began telling us the story of his troubled past. At age sixteen he'd fallen in with the wrong crowd in his hometown of Greenwood, South Carolina, and had spent a year in a reformatory. When he was released he'd had good intentions, but because of his record, he couldn't find a job.

He became desperate and decided to rob a local service station so he could have enough money to leave the state. He stole his father's car and gun and just before closing time drove up to the service window of a gasoline station. He was about to demand all the money from the woman manager.

"But just then," he explained, "I looked up and saw the sign overhead. It read, 'GOD IS OUR SECURITY GUARD—ALWAYS ON THE JOB.' And I knew I couldn't rob that place. I then rushed home and prayed all night. I was determined to get my life straightened out. And with God's help, I did."

As he finished, I looked at my husband. Both of us remembered a night thirteen years ago when I sat at our kitchen table in the same town of Greenwood, South Carolina, trying to make a sign for our business. I had scribbled down several words. Then finally it came, the slogan that my husband put on the sign that stood on the roof of the small service station that we managed:

GOD IS OUR SECURITY GUARD—ALWAYS ON THE JOB.

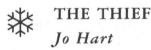

THE THIEF
Jo Hart

After years of wandering, Clint Dennis had come to that point in his life when he knew he had been missing something important. And for months he had felt he could find what that something was in that church on the hillside in North Phoenix.

He arrived at Phoenix First Assembly of God on an unusual day. The choir room was filled with members putting on long robes, tying ropes around their waists, wrapping headdresses around their heads. "Come be part of the mob," a stranger told him.

It was Palm Sunday and the church was reenacting the Crucifixion in costume. Like others in the congregation, he would be part of the crowd that yelled, "Crucify Him! Crucify Him!" Hesitantly he agreed.

Then another stranger hurried up to him. "The man who was supposed to play one of the thieves on the cross didn't show up," he said. "Would you take his place?"

Again he agreed and was shown to the cross where he would look on as Christ died. Just then, though, something about Clint's manner caught a member's eye. He turned to Clint and asked, "Have you ever asked Jesus to forgive your sins?"

"No," Clint replied softly, "but that's why I came here." There beneath the cross, they prayed, and Clint asked Jesus to come into his heart. His life was transformed.

What the church didn't know then was that Clint had been in prison for ten years. Even after his release he had gone on stealing cars and trucks until he knew he had been missing something in life. He was a real thief, but at last he was welcomed into God's kingdom by the same Jesus who welcomed another thief two thousand years ago.

 ## A THING OF BEAUTY
Kenneth Lynch

Years ago, before I moved my metalworking to Connecticut, I had a shop on the West Side of Manhattan—any farther west and you'd get your feet wet. One day an elderly woman came in. When she asked if we could make a chalice for her, I was ready to shake my head.

In the first place, judging from her threadbare coat and her work-gnarled hands, I felt sure she couldn't afford such a costly piece. Such works, as used in serving Holy Communion, are usually handcrafted out of silver and plated with gold. And I didn't have the heart to tell her how much one would cost.

But then, the Gaelic lilt in her voice reminded me of my own great aunt from Ireland. And when she explained that as the mother of a large family, all now grown and dispersed, she wanted the chalice as a gift for her youngest son, shortly to be ordained as a priest, my heart melted.

"How much . . . ?" she ventured. "How much would ye say such a thing would cost?" Reaching inside her coat she withdrew a roll of worn one-dollar bills.

"I've saved through the years for this," she said, lifting her chin a bit, "and I have eighty-five dollars. Will it be enough?"

I was in a dilemma. The bottom price for a handwrought chalice in those days was $150. But she was so hopeful.

"We can do it for seventy-five dollars," I said.

Her eyes lighted up and she pressed all the bills on me. "Take it all," she said, "and make it twice as good. Nothing will be too fine for my youngest on his great day."

"We'll do our best," I promised.

As she walked out of the shop, I turned to see one of our silversmiths who had been standing in the back watching us.

This man was a fine craftsman. He had come to America from
Ireland but had learned his art in France. When he worked he
was superb, but he couldn't stay away from the bottle. Things
had come to the point that I knew I would have to let him go,
but now, seeing him, I had a strange feeling that I must give
him this one last job.

Calling him up, I told him what the woman wanted and in a
meaningful way added, "Now do the best you can."

He nodded and went to his bench.

I prayed that he'd stick to his work and have the chalice ready
in time.

The Lord heard my prayer, for the silversmith worked hard
on it, often until late at night. There were no more days when
he'd phone in "sick" or be in such poor control of himself that I
couldn't trust him to forge a hinge. I was surprised at the
change in him, and when I'd compliment him on the job he was
doing, he'd only give a quick nod and go on with his work.

The chalice was finished—on time—and the silversmith
brought it to me for my approval. He stood before me straight
and proud. His eyes were clear and forthright as he held up the
cup, beautifully wrought in gold-plated silver.

"Well done!" I said enthusiastically. "Well done."

He then went out and bought a handsome case of polished
walnut. He lined it himself with fine deep-blue velvet and
placed the chalice inside.

When the old woman returned, I presented her with the case.
She lifted the lid and gasped.

"Oh . . . oh, it is so beautiful . . . so beautiful!" Then she
looked up questioningly. "Are you sure, Mr. Lynch, that
eighty-five dollars is enough?"

"Of course, Mother," I said, patting her shoulder. And I
meant it. She left the shop thanking "the mighty Lord."

Unfortunately the silversmith wasn't in the shop at the time,
but when he came in later, I told him how pleased she had been.
"That was a wonderful thing you did," I said, taking his hand.
"You made a woman very, very happy."

He looked at me for a moment. "It was something I had to
do, Mr. Lynch," he said finally. "You see, that woman—she is
my mother."

"But why didn't you—?"

"I've thrown my life away, Mr. Lynch. You know that as well

as I do. When I was a boy I ran away to sea. Never once did I
write home. Now I didn't want my mother to see the drunk her
son has become. It's better this way . . . until I can be sure of
myself."

The next day the silversmith quickly packed his few belong-
ings and left the shop. I never saw him again. But I feel in my
heart that he went on to do well. For the mother's love for one of
her sons touched the life of another in a way she could never
have imagined.

 ## FLOWERS IN TIME
Ellen St. John Barnwell

"Speak to me, Lord, and speak through me." It was my daily
prayer and I said it that Sunday at St. Luke's. On the altar, red
roses glowed, roses I'd provided in memory of my mother.
When the service was over, I turned to my son, Bob. "After we
have dinner, let's take the altar flowers to Miss Marie."

"Good idea," he agreed. Mother and Miss Marie, now in her
eighties, had been close friends.

Driving home, humming the recessional hymn together, we
broke off at the same moment. "Let's take the flowers to Miss
Marie right now." The identical thought had occurred to both
of us.

"What made you change your mind?" I asked as Bob turned
the car toward Miss Marie's house.

"I don't know," was all he could say.

"I don't either." I hesitated. "But let's not waste any time."

Miss Marie's daughter, Alice, answered the doorbell. "How
nice!" she said as I handed her the roses. "I've been in bed with
the flu." She gestured vaguely. "Mother was resting in her
room. Let me see if she's awake now."

Then, a sharp cry.

Bob and I raced down the hall. Miss Marie lay unconscious on
the floor. Bob lifted her to her bed. I dialed the emergency
ambulance. Alice began sponging Miss Marie's forehead with
cool water. Her eyes fluttered.

"Lucky you got to her in time," the medic told us. "When it's a little stroke they can't call for help."

"Couldn't speak," Miss Marie murmured. "Prayed to God in my heart."

That made two prayers He'd answered loud and clear.

PRAYER FOR TOMORROW
—*Carlene A. Wallace*

Beyond today will be tomorrow,
But what it will bring of joy or sorrow
I cannot know. I only pray
Your guidance, Lord, each hour, each day,
Your strength to bear whatever may be
Your loving wisdom has for me.
So sweet or bitter, sad or gay,
Be with me, Lord, beyond today.

THE COLUMN OF SMOKE
Joseph Caldwell

I was waiting for the bus to take me down from the Janiculum Hill into the city of Rome when I turned and saw black smoke rising into the sky. It seemed to be coming from my studio, a small, cabinlike study built up against the ancient Roman wall that bounded the grounds of the American Academy. I'd arrived there three weeks before with my most precious possession: the first draft of my new novel.

The smoke—I thought of the electric coil I'd been using to heat water for the endless cups of tea I need to fuel my writing. What if I had started heating water and forgotten. Suppose the coil had slipped from the cup and started a fire that would not only destroy the studio committed to my care for a year but the pages and pages of work I could never duplicate.

I hurried back, but soon saw that the smoke came from a bonfire in the adjoining orchard. I felt relieved, and even a little foolish. But since I was now so close, I went into my studio anyway.

The electric coil *was* still plugged in, and the water I'd meant to use for tea before I left had all boiled out of a cup that had tipped over—and the red-hot coil had toppled onto the desk and was charring the wood. Manuscript pages that would have flared up in a second were only inches away.

Drawn by that column of smoke, I'd come back just in time. "Thank God," I said.

Of course, thank God.

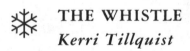

THE WHISTLE
Kerri Tillquist

I was packing that morning when I heard a shrill whistle. I rushed into the living room only to discover it came from the TV. We were preparing to go from Boulder to Montrose, Colorado, with our ten-week-old baby, Leslie.

As we drove through the mountains that afternoon, big sleety drops of rain turned into heavy wet flakes of snow. Near the top of Fremont Pass, traffic slowed and we could barely see. I nursed Leslie and then Neil pulled over and held her. "Is something wrong?" I asked when Leslie's cry suddenly became low and husky.

Neil handed her back to me in a panic. She was coughing and gasping. I patted her on the back, but she turned bluish gray and seemed to stop breathing. I began to administer mouth-to-mouth resuscitation, but without oxygen she could go into respiratory arrest. "Lord," I prayed, "save my baby."

Just then the shrill sound of a whistle pierced the swirling snow. "That's a mine over there," I called to Neil. "Someone will have oxygen there."

Neil started the car and crossed the road to the gate of a molybdenum mine. We flagged a guard, told him our problem, then raced down the drive, where two nurses met us with an oxygen tank. I put the huge mask over Leslie's ashen face and, slowly, she began breathing again.

Later we went to a hospital, where tests confirmed that Leslie was all right. The doctor there had one question: "How did you know there would be oxygen at the mine?"

The shrill sound I had heard that morning was a mine whistle blowing in an episode of *The Waltons*. I watched just long enough to see a miner revived—with oxygen.

THE SKUNK
Elizabeth Sherrill

It was a rustling in the woods that made me glance out the window beside my word processor. At the edge of the trees I caught sight of a skunk, his black-and-white pattern echoing the dappled light. He seemed to be furiously busy—burrowing maybe? My knowledge of skunks began and ended with that appalling odor.

Next moment, though, the animal emerged from beneath the trees and ran zigzagging across the lawn: plumelike tail, striped back and . . . where his head should have been, a bizarre-looking yellow helmet. As he came closer I saw what the "helmet" was. A six-ounce plastic yogurt container.

The carton struck a rock, and the creature whirled in another direction, only to bump up against our picnic table. For a second he stood still, shaking his head frantically. But the yogurt carton was cone-shaped, the narrow mouth wedged fast about his neck. The skunk charged blindly back into the woods.

I stared after him in dismay. How long since he had forced his head into that carton to reach some bit of food on the bottom? How long had he been running in darkness and terror?

It would be the work of a second for me, I thought, to pull that thing off. But the idea of pursuing a skunk through the undergrowth kept me immobilized at the window. How would I ever catch him? And then what? In his panic wouldn't he be certain to spray me?

I sat down and tried to pick up the thread of the story due in the mail that afternoon. But I could think only of an animal running till he dropped from exhaustion. Mustn't this sort of thing have happened before? Might animal experts know what to do?

From the kitchen telephone I dialed the local ASPCA. "We only handle domestic animals," the woman told me. "You want the State Conservation Department." She gave me a number in New Paltz, New York.

New Paltz meant a toll call. Anyhow, by now the skunk would be a long way off. Maybe someone else would see him. Someone braver and more athletic.

I dialed the number in New Paltz. A man in the Department of Wildlife listened to my story, then held a muffled conversation. "As long as skunks can't see you," he said into the phone, "they don't spray."

Well . . . that sounded all right, as long as the skunk's head was inside the container. "What happens after the carton comes off?" I asked.

"Just make sure," the man advised, "that he doesn't feel threatened."

I wondered how one went about reassuring a terrified skunk.

"You could throw a blanket over him," Wildlife suggested. "Then run while he's finding his way out."

"That might work," I said, but I must have sounded as unsure as I felt, because the man asked where I was calling from and began looking up names of conservation officers in my area.

How long would it take, I wondered, for someone to get here? Where would the skunk be by then? Standing there in the kitchen, I was gripped by a sudden strange urgency. I thanked the man, hung up, and ran outside. Without stopping to change out of my next-to-best slacks (*does skunk scent ever wash out?*), and forgetting about the blanket theory, I ran up our driveway to the road.

Of course the skunk wasn't there. Nor did I know why I was. In his frenzy, when I'd seen him last, the animal had been heading the opposite way, straight down the hill into the woods.

But my feet never slowed. I turned left and dashed down the street as though rushing to a long-ordained appointment. I'd run perhaps a hundred yards when a black-and-white streak emerged from the bushes beside the road and ran straight at me, the carton bumping the pavement with each step. I stooped down and grabbed hold of the yogurt carton before the astonishment of finding the skunk hit me.

The animal was tugging and twisting, unexpectedly strong, to get away. *If they can't see you they won't spray.* His front claws scrabbled against the slippery yellow plastic, his body strained backward, and still he could not wrench free of the carton's viselike neck. It took both of my hands tugging the other way to hold on—until a small black head suddenly popped free.

And there we stood, facing each other, two feet apart.

I don't know what *he* saw, and how threatening or not the apparition was, but what *I* saw was a sharp quivering nose, two small round ears, and alert black eyes that stared straight into mine.

For fully ten seconds we held each other's gaze. Then the skunk turned, ran a few yards, and vanished into the mouth of a culvert that runs beneath the road.

For a moment more I stood there, looking after him. Three minutes could not have passed since I hung up the telephone in the kitchen.

But a timeless parable had played itself out, I thought, as I headed back down the drive. The skunk was all those needs I hesitate to get involved in: *Involvement takes time and I have deadlines to meet. I probably can't do anything anyway. Somebody else can handle it better. Besides, involvement can be ugly, and the stench may rub off on me.*

And all these things, of course, may be true. But I've got a yellow pencil-holder on my desk, a rather scratched and battered one, to remind me that every now and then God's answer to a need is me.

MISSION TO THE STRANGEST PLACE
Bruce E. Olson

Looking back on it, I can see how people viewed me as a religious crackpot. I got off the plane in Caracas, Venezuela, that hot August day back in 1962 with only seventy-two dollars in my pocket, nineteen years old, alone, unable to speak Spanish, but convinced that the Lord had told me to go to South America and preach His word to the Indians.

It had all started four years earlier, back in St. Paul, Minnesota, when Jesus Christ became very real to me. My relationship with Him deepened in college, where my aim was to become a professor of languages. However, I began to feel this inner nudge to share His life with those who had never known Him.

"But where, Lord?" I found myself asking.

Then over a period of time, I became interested in South America, particularly Venezuela and Colombia.

I applied to a well-known mission board in Venezuela. They informed me that I didn't have the educational requirements. I was relieved and returned to my dream of becoming a language professor.

Yet God still nudged me.

"But, Lord, I was turned down. I have no contacts, no money, no mission board. You want me to go down there by myself without anyone to take care of me?"

And ever so gently in my mind, the words came, "Bruce, I'm in South America too."

Then came that wonderful feeling of reassurance. Suddenly I knew that with Him by my side I could do anything. But I soon discovered the big difference between plunging ahead on your own power and waiting for His guidance. The Lord knew how inadequate I was. And His preparation came in a series of remarkable incidents.

Soon after I arrived in Caracas, so alone and so ill-equipped, a Venezuelan college student noticed me wandering about the city. We struck up a friendship and I moved into his house where I began to learn the language.

When he learned of my interest in the Indians, he introduced me to a doctor with the government's Indian Commission. Doctor Christian invited me to accompany him by canoe up the muddy Orinoco River. For three weeks I lived with a semi-civilized tribe and learned their ways.

After this trip, the doctor referred me to an American-Venezuelan cultural exchange program in Caracas where I met a man with the Ministry of Health. He asked me to teach English to some university students preparing to attend Harvard University's school of tropical medicine. I did, and at the same time I learned the rudiments of tropical medicine.

One day my superior and I were talking about Indians. "Have you ever heard of the Motilone tribe?" he asked. He described a legendary Stone Age tribe that had resisted civilization since time began. No one had ever learned their language, since few entering their territory ever returned.

These fierce savages, he said, lived in a wild jungle area on the border between Venezuela and Colombia.

Venezuela and Colombia!

I sank back in awe. I knew then that those were the people to whom God wanted me to go.

Within a week I was on a bus headed for the foothills of the Andes Mountains. Then I set off into the jungle alone. Three days later I stumbled half-starved into a settlement of Yucco Indians, a semiprimitive tribe. For eight months I lived with them, learning their language. Finally three Yucco braves reluctantly agreed to take me to a trail that led to the Motilones.

We chopped our way through the jungle for seven days. Suddenly an arrow pierced my thigh. I fell to the ground; my companions fled.

Out of the ferns stepped five squat brown men, eyes glittering under short-cropped hair. I had met the Motilones.

They dragged me to my feet and I limped with them to their settlement. I was thrust into a communal hut where I lay on a palm mat. Days went by; my wound festered. I developed amoebic dysentery and began hemorrhaging blood.

The period that followed was a nightmare of pain and trial. However, I continued to try to bring God's love to those people. Finally, some of them took pity on me and one in particular, a man called Bobarishora, became my friend. As they tried to pronounce my name, "Bruce" became "Bruchko," which has stayed with me ever since.

Meanwhile a powerful chieftain who lived in a distant village heard of me and wanted to kill me. Now I felt impelled to visit this chieftain. If I could gain his friendship, I could travel safely throughout all Motilone territory. My native friends shook their heads but I insisted. However, during the trip to see this chief, I became terribly fatigued.

Suddenly Bobarishora looked at me and gasped, "Bruchko, your eyes have turned yellow!"

I had hepatitis. My only hope was to continue on and trust in God.

The chief was waiting in a frenzy. "Why have you not killed him?"

My friends argued that I was dying already. Later I learned that to a Motilone the worst thing is to die outside your own land. Then your soul is doomed to wander forever.

The chief agreed this would be a fitting end for me. For two weeks I lay in a hut slowly dying. There was little sound except the low murmur of women as they worked.

Suddenly the voices rose in alarm. I heard the distant drone of a helicopter. My friend, Bobarishora, rushed to my side. "Bruchko, the cannibal flute is coming."

The Motilones felt that airplanes were droning flutes of the whiteskins who, they believed, were cannibals who ate Motilones. "Bobby," I pleaded, "carry me out and put a red cloth next to me." He pulled me to a clearing, then fled.

Now I could hear the helicopter land and soon I was looking up into the amazed face of a doctor I had met when I first traveled up the Orinoco River. He explained that he had been visiting an oil company camp. On impulse he asked their pilot to fly him over Motilone territory to take pictures.

I was taken to Maracaibo where I was told it would be six months before I would recover and that I could never return to a jungle climate. But I had a deepening peace in my heart. God had brought me to the Motilones; He would help me to continue. Within three weeks I was back up the river, well supplied with medicines given me by an oil company.

The Motilone chief received me with awe. To him the helicopter had been a sacred vulture sent to take my body. Now I had returned with supernatural prestige. I lived with the Motilones, learning their language, their customs.

But the witch doctors watched me with suspicion. I knew that Motilones believed that evil spirits lived in rocks, trees, and rivers. So one day I placed a smear of river mud under my microscope and showed it to a witch doctor.

"There," I said, referring to the wriggling microbes, "are your evil spirits."

She shrank back in terror. Then I showed her how disinfectant left them lifeless. This is how I first introduced the Motilones to medical science. It was also how their witch doctors became my close allies.

I lived with them for four years, but when I felt ready to give the Motilones the word of God I felt confused and frustrated. They had a vague belief in an entity "who lived somewhere," but where they did not know. Yet how could I introduce God as He really was, independent of my own personality and culture?

I searched for some illustration as a key in introducing the Bible; to them a book was meaningless. I prayed that God would speak through me, that He would show me the right time to do it.

One afternoon the answer came. As Bobarishora, some other men, and I were out walking, we heard agonizing cries echoing through the valley. We looked for their source and found Atabadora, a powerful tribal leader. He had dug a deep pit and was now calling into it for their god to reveal himself. Atabadora's brother had died in a strange territory and he wanted assurance that his brother's spirit would be brought back.

Another man perched in the top of a tall tree was shouting for the great spirit "to come from the horizon." The two had been screaming since sunrise, and as evening shadows crept over them, their voices had dwindled to a croak.

I now found it possible to start a lively discussion. The man in the tree came down and joined us. He reminded us of the tribal legend about the tall man who one day would walk through the tribe carrying a banana stalk out of which God would come.

"Why look for God in a banana stalk?" I asked in puzzlement.

They couldn't explain it. Bobarishora walked over to a banana tree, cut off a cross section, and tossed it to us. "This is the kind of banana stalk our god can come from."

In a mirthful mood, one of the other men struck at the stalk with his machete, hitting it lengthwise.

I gasped.

As it split open, the pale unborn banana leaves unpeeled from within it like the pages of a book.

And now I understood the reason for each step God had had me take in the four years of getting to know the Motilones, of mastering each nuance of their strange and beautiful tongue, of learning how they thought, their hopes and dreams.

I grabbed up my pack and took out my Bible. Flipping open the pages, I pointed to its leaves and said, "This is it. God's language is here. This is God's banana stalk!"

GOD

Supplies

OUR NEEDS

But my God shall supply all your need according to his riches in glory by Christ Jesus.

—PHILIPPIANS 4:19

WHAT TO PRAY FOR
—*James A. Bowman*

> I asked for bread and got a stone;
> I used the stone to grind the grain
> That made the flour to form the bread
> That I could not obtain.
>
> Instead of asking Him to give
> The things for which we pray,
> All that we need to ask from God
> Is this: show us the way.

 ## SUDDEN INCREASE
Esther McIntosh

I had only two one-dollar bills in my wallet and they had to last until payday, ten days away. My husband was away on business, and I was at home with our two children conserving every cent.

On Monday my father called to say he needed to attend a union meeting on Friday afternoon. Would I come and stay with Mother? She was bedridden with brain cancer and had to have someone help her with her medicine. I didn't hesitate to say yes. Back then, in 1970, one dollar would buy enough gas to get there and back, and I would still have an "emergency" dollar left.

All week long my five-year-old kept asking for a treat from the ice cream truck. And each time, I would open my wallet, show her the two one-dollar bills, and explain why we couldn't afford such a luxury.

When we arrived on Friday, Daddy's parting words were, "Don't forget to give Mom her Dilantin," her anticonvulsant medicine. But after he'd gone I discovered the bottle was empty. I was terrified that if Mother didn't get her medicine on time, she'd go into convulsions.

Mother told me to check her purse and a couple of other places for loose change, but that was all I found—loose change. I telephoned my sisters, but no one was home. The prescription cost over eight dollars. Where would I get that money?

"God will take care of it," Mother said.

At my wit's end, I decided to go to the pharmacist's with my lone dollar and beg him to trust me for the rest. But when I looked in my wallet again, I was stunned.

That single was a ten-dollar bill.

 ## THE LITTLE RED HEN
Josephine M. Kuntz

At one point during the winter of 1940, my husband, a house painter, was temporarily unemployed because of the weather, and the textile plant where I worked was closed due to a seasonal lay-off. We literally had no money. To make matters worse, our eighteen-month-old daughter, Rachel, was recovering poorly from pneumonia, and the doctor insisted we feed her a boiled egg each day. Even that was beyond our means.

"Why not pray for an egg?" suggested our baby-sitter, who was staying on without pay to help us. We were a churchgoing family, but this teenager's depth of faith was something new to us at the time. All the same, she and I got on our knees and told the Lord that Rachel needed an egg each morning. We left the problem in His hands.

About ten o'clock that morning we heard some cackling coming from the hedge fence in front of our house. There among the bare branches sat a fat red hen. We had no idea where she had come from. We just watched in amazement as she laid an egg and then proceeded down the road, out of sight.

The little red hen that first day was a surprise, and we thanked God for it, but can you imagine how startled we were when we heard the hen cackling in the hedge the next morning? And the morning after that, and the morning after that? Every day for over a week, Rachel had a fresh boiled egg.

Rachel grew better and better, and at last the weather turned and my husband went back to work. The next morning I waited by the window and watched. But our prayers had been answered—precisely.

The little red hen did not come back. Ever.

 ## AT A CROSSROAD
Irma Burrill

I couldn't bear the thought of leaving California. After twenty-two years of being moved all around the country, I felt we'd found a home in Merced. Now my husband, Chuck, had retired from the Air Force and was planning to settle us back in Illinois, where we'd both grown up. He felt we should be near our families. I felt we'd put down new roots right where we were; our home, our church, and our friends were in California.

For weeks I had been struggling with the decision as I ferried children about in my job as an elementary school bus driver. That was another thing: I loved my job, I loved the kids, and I even loved the big yellow school bus. So, as the final day of school drew near, I began to wish I hadn't agreed to move, and I pleaded with God: "Please change Chuck's mind."

But Chuck's mind was made up. And before I knew it, the last day of school arrived—my last day as a bus driver.

"Well, this is it, Lord," I whispered that afternoon as I prepared for the routine safety check. I slipped the rubber mallet out of its boot and gave the old bus an affectionate pat on the side as I circled around, thumping each of the tires to check for proper inflation. Then I climbed onto the driver's seat, ready to pick up the kids for the last time.

And all the while I prayed, "Lord, I still don't want to leave all this, but You haven't told me what You want."

So far He hadn't answered.

As I sat waiting for school to let out, I kept mulling over all the reasons for staying. Our three boys had so taken to life in California. They had paper routes, girlfriends, a pet desert tortoise. I thought of the good times we'd had overhauling motorcycles on the living room carpet and sleeping on the roof of our station wagon to study the stars.

The people at church were like family. The church nursery had been my second home for several years, and the Bible study I was in seemed tailor-made for me. And Chuck, why, he was a trustee, a deacon, an usher—he'd even helped put a roof on the church.

"Bus driver," came a child's timid voice, "would you like some candy?" I looked down to see a grubby hand shoving a dripping glob of melted chocolate toward me. I gulped. I'd learned a long time ago that to refuse would be to break a little one's heart.

"Thank you, Maria," I said, smiling as I scooped up the brown mass from the grimy palm. Her face beamed as I poured it into my mouth.

How I loved these little guys and gals, with their jars of caterpillars and ladybugs, the limp roses and half-eaten apples, the hugs, the tears, the nosebleeds, the "Tie my shoe" and "Gee, bus driver, you're older'n my dad!"

As I drove down Bear Creek Drive, I thought of the many times I'd asked God to lift my spirits and He'd sent a covey of baby quail scurrying across the highway, or some kit foxes romping on the hills.

I dropped off the last little guy and watched him wave good-bye to me, appearing as downcast as I was. I swallowed hard and shifted into gear. "I know how you feel, little guy," I sighed.

Back at my reserved space in the bus barn, I switched off the engine and sat for a long moment in the driver's seat, fighting back tears. I had to get it over with. I made my last entry in the log book, then picked up the broom and cleaning cloth from the storage chest under the rear seat.

One by one I turned up the seat cushions, picked up debris, and wiped the seats clean as I worked my way toward the front of the bus. But all the while, I kept wondering why God had seemed so silent to me. I thought He *always* answered prayer.

I stooped to pick up a scrap of cardboard, a piece of a jigsaw puzzle that had fallen face down on the floor. *What good is a puzzle with a piece missing?* I mused.

Then I turned it over and caught my breath. Even in the ninety-degree heat I felt goose bumps springing up all over my body. My downcast spirit began to revive. How could I have doubted? God had answered my prayer after all.

For there in the palm of my hand lay a tiny map of the state of Illinois.

 ## MORELS IN THE GARDEN
Sandra Fischer

That spring, for the first time in years, Mother couldn't go mushrooming. After surgery, she was recuperating at our home. No scurrying off to the moist Hoosier woodlands. No hunting for morels, the rare coneshaped mushrooms that grow for a short time every spring.

For Mother that was a real hardship; mushrooming was her gift. Every year we kids would go into the woods with her; we'd fan out in different directions, searching in proven morel breeding grounds such as patches of mayapple, rotting stumps, and fallen elm trees. But it was always Mother who would call out suddenly, "Come quick! Look what I've found." And there, in an unpromising pile of decaying leaves, half-hidden, would be the precious honeycomb spikes of morels we'd been seeking.

"These mushrooms are like the manna that God sent the children of Israel in the wilderness," Mother would say. "He chooses when and where He wants them to appear."

That spring, Mother longed to go again to the woods where the morels grew, but forced to stay near home, she puttered listlessly in the garden.

Then one Saturday, Mother was watering the tulips outside the living room window when I heard her cry, "Come quick! Look what I've found."

There among the yellow tulips I spotted something familiar —a cone-shaped morel. We scanned the ground to find another one, and another, growing where they never had grown before —and never have since.

A RIFLE AND A SOLDIER'S PRAYER

Adolf Zinsser, as told to John and
Elizabeth Sherrill

I was barely six years old when the conversation around our dining room table began to revolve around a man named Adolf Hitler. Dinner came in the middle of the day, and there were always fifteen to twenty people present, including workmen from the water-powered flour mill that had been in our family for six generations. I can see them now, trooping in from work, still white with flour even after a scrubbing.

The talk about Hitler didn't start right away. First came Scripture reading and prayer. But when the Bible was put on the sideboard and the covers came off the steaming tureens, the excited discussions would begin. Times had been hard in Germany for many years. But Hitler was going to change all that, the grown-ups said. His latest radio address would be discussed point by point.

Papa noted that when Hitler talked about his plans, he would always add, ". . . insofar as the Almighty will help us." It was always *the Almighty*, never *God*, but still . . . "He sounds like a believer," Mama agreed.

Later, of course, Hitler's true colors came out. He began an unstated campaign against any loyalty other than to himself—especially among the young. At the age of ten I had to start attending *Jungvolk* meetings; these "happened" to be scheduled on Sunday mornings, right at church time. At fourteen I graduated to the Hitler Youth. Sunday after Sunday I'd put on my brown shirt and get on my bike and pedal off to march and sing and swear undying allegiance to the Führer.

My parents said little to me about their misgivings—to do so would put us all in danger. Occasionally, though, their feelings would show through. By this time every business letter had to close with the words *Heil Hitler*. One day my father and I were alone in the mill office as he went through his mail. "In this family," he burst out suddenly, "we don't say 'Heil Hitler!' We say, 'Heil Jesus!' "

But though they seldom put their feelings into words, my parents' actions spoke for them. Every Sunday evening a group met for worship in our home. One day the police arrived to

enforce a new law closing such independent churches and confis-
cating their property. They carted away the hymn books, the
portable pulpit, the banner saying "Jesus is Lord," even the
broom Mama used to get the room ready for the meeting.

"The Führer is not against religion," the police chief read
from the new regulations. "You may continue to meet, but
never in groups of more than three."

My father and mother did not hesitate. They shifted the now-
illegal worship services to the mill, where the roar of the water
and the clank of machinery drowned out the songs and prayers.

I was fifteen years old now and tall for my age, blond and
blue-eyed, the very type Hitler associated with his fantasies of a
"master race"—and the kind he wanted for his elite SS. Sure
enough, one day an SS team arrived in our small town of
Plüderhausen, seeking recruits. A dozen of us boys were driven
to a nearby castle, where we were met by an SS officer, splendid
in gleaming boots, braided epaulets, and soft-crowned cap. He
set our pulses pounding as he described the glorious exploits of
his unit in the liberation of neighboring lands. Stressing the
honor being done us, he urged us to enlist then and there.

However, I did not understand the resistance rising within
me. To a youngster of fifteen brought up on Nazi doctrine, as
sensitive to peer pressure as any teenager, everything this dash-
ing hero-figure said seemed undeniable. Yet I felt a need for
caution. Was it my parents' prayers? Again they said little—
but I knew they prayed for me every day. And in the secret
church meeting in the mill, we sang that "prayer removes
mountains."

I refused to volunteer. The officer told me I did not love my
country and called me a coward. I knew the first was not true
and I hoped the second was not true. But still I would not join
the SS.

Two years passed, years of growing loneliness. I was seventeen, enrolled in millers' school, when in the spring of 1944,
along with other teenagers and men too infirm to have been
called up before, I was drafted into the army. The fact that the
military was making do with such unpromising material would
have alerted wiser heads to the fact that Hitler's Thousand-Year
Reich was in trouble. But our radio and newspapers carried only
accounts of victory.

My first night in basic-training camp, the other draftees rode me when I brought out my Bible. "You're crazy," one boy mocked. "That's just the Jews' book of lies. In a few years no one will read it anymore. We'll all be reading *Mein Kampf*."

From then on, when I wanted to talk to God, I'd go out into the fields, or find an empty storeroom, or pull the blanket over my head at night. Maybe the SS officer had been right when he called me a coward.

At the camp, we were taught to shoot. Our rifles, the sergeant told us, would be everything to us. He warned us never, never to lose the ones we were about to be issued. Anyone who did would be court-martialed. Only after this speech did he hand out our rifles, writing down the serial number in the *Soldbuch* that every soldier had to carry.

To my great surprise I turned out to be an excellent shot. When the instructor collected the paper targets from the firing range, mine would always have the highest score. I was tremendously proud. It wasn't until one night during my prayer time that I began to think about the purpose of all this practice. Suppose that were not a piece of paper in the sights of my rifle, but a man . . .

I thought about my father and mother and their remnant church—mostly women and old men now—meeting three times a week in the noisy mill, risking arrest, which had already happened to some of our Christian friends. "Lord Jesus," I prayed beneath my blanket, "let me never kill a man for a government that makes people hide to worship You."

In May 1944, after a mere two weeks of training, we raw recruits were sent to the French coast to help man Hitler's "impregnable" Atlantic wall. My unit was assigned to a bunker in Normandy, just east of the River Seine. We had been told that our air force would support us if the Allies were so foolish as to attempt an invasion. But although Allied planes flew overhead often, we saw no German ones.

In early June the Allied bombing raids increased. On the night of June 5 the sky throbbed with more planes than I dreamed existed. Toward morning we saw shell flashes in the distance and realized there must be ships offshore. By daylight the rumors were confirmed: the "impossible" invasion had begun.

Our sector was not hit in the initial assault, and our confidence remained high. Each night we climbed out of the bunker and stood scanning the skies. Surely this was the time when the Führer would launch his Secret Weapon!

In mid-June we left the coast and began a tactical maneuver back up the Seine. Not a retreat, our officers stressed — a strategic repositioning for the counteroffensive the Führer would soon be mounting. Now that we were billeted on French farms rather than in fortified bunkers, our wariness over our rifles increased. Each night we placed them beneath the straw we used for beds — each man sleeping on top of his weapon.

Although the din of battle was all around us, our unit had so far done no fighting. Across the Seine, as we moved upriver, we occasionally caught sight of a gray-green tank with a white star on the side. Americans. Once we saw German soldiers struggling toward us across the river, some paddling inflated rafts, others swimming, weapons abandoned. Why didn't Hitler unleash the Secret Weapon?

And then one day tanks opened fire at us from across the river. We scrambled into the fields. I crouched in some waist-high wheat, ran through an apple orchard, stumbled past an area marked LAND MINES, and ran some more.

That night, I joined a unit made up of men from other scattered companies. From then on I moved with such makeshift groups, stopping at a farmhouse for a night or a week, sleeping on my rifle. Although I had now been fired at a number of times, no unit that I'd been with had yet been in a position to return the fire. Was God answering my prayer that I never shoot at a human being?

One night we bedded down in a great stone barn with sentries posted outside. I shaped a pallet of straw, placed my rifle beneath it as usual, and lay down, as always, right on top. Next morning when the corporal roused us we groped under the straw to retrieve our rifles, then lined up stiffly for inspection.

Except me. I was still on hands and knees sifting through my little heap of straw.

"On your feet, soldier!" the corporal barked. "With your rifle!" he snapped as I obeyed.

"I—it—" I stammered. "It's not here!"

"What do you mean, 'not here'?"

I gestured helplessly at the scattered straw. "It was there last night, right underneath me. Only—now it's not."

The entire unit searched that barn from end to end. Those who'd slept nearest me confirmed that I'd placed the weapon where I said. The corporal checked every rifle in the barn against the number in my *Soldbuch*. No other soldier had taken it—and no one from outside could have got in past the guards. How could a rifle disappear into thin air?

The corporal was fuming. Our orders were to march out, and I'd delayed us all! Nor was there a spare rifle to give me. Our troops were short of everything—ammunition, weapons, medicine. All that day we marched, followed by our horse-drawn supply cart, while I saw myself standing in front of a firing squad, my parents getting the news . . .

Late that same afternoon we engaged in our first exchange of fire. The Allies were on the other side of a small valley. Our squad took cover and began firing. Except me. With no rifle to shoot, I was put in charge of the terrified horse. As bullets whined around us I tried to calm the panicky animal, though I was easily as frightened as he.

It wasn't until that night, reading my Bible in a solitary corner of yet another barn, that I realized what had happened. That day, for the first time, the order had come to shoot. That day, for the first time, I had been unable to obey.

For the next several days I marched and bivouacked and carried equipment, but I never fired a weapon because I did not have one. The threat of court-martial hung heavy over me, but we were regrouping too often for official procedures to be followed through.

One morning in July my current unit was approaching a bridge when two Canadians armed with submachine guns jumped up on either side of the road.

"Halt! Hands up!"

Our lieutenant had an automatic pistol, which he let drop as he raised his hands. The rest of us threw our rifles clattering to the ground. All, of course, except me.

The mystery of the missing rifle was never solved. I spent the final ten months of the war as a prisoner in England, working on a farm owned by a family that reminded me a lot of my own. I worried about my parents, of course, as the Allied forces pushed on into Germany and the fighting drew near to Plüderhausen. All I could do was pray that they be kept safe (and they were!), as they had prayed for me.

Praying was a lot, though. That was a truth I learned at age seventeen, groping about in some straw on a stone floor. Prayer can indeed remove mountains— and rifles too.

 ## WHEN THE LIGHTS CAME ON
Franklin Graham

In 1971, as a newly licensed pilot, I was flying with my flight instructor from Vero Beach, Florida, to Longview, Texas. That night, we hit bad weather over Mobile, Alabama, and air-traffic controllers suggested we fly north toward Jackson, Mississippi, to avoid an approaching storm.

As we rose above the clouds, I noticed the instrument panel lights flicker. A minute later, radios and instruments started going dead; then all our lights went out. Our situation was desperate, and as we flew an emergency triangle, we prayed to God for His protection. We decided to drop below the clouds and try to see the ground. Soon we spotted the distant lights of Jackson and headed for the airport's rotating beacon.

We circled the control tower twice, then got a green light to land. Without any electrical power, we had to lower the landing gear manually. At that moment, all the strobe landing lights came on and slowly, safely we touched ground.

Then the landing lights went off. *That's odd,* I thought, *at least they could have waited until we taxied to the ramp.* It was even odder when a man from the tower asked us, "Who gave you permission to land?"

And then, little by little, we learned that no one in the tower had seen us circling overhead. The green light had been flashed by a traffic controller who was explaining to his visiting pastor what he would do in case a plane ever attempted to land without radio communication. The emergency landing lights were part of the same demonstration.

But the whole story can never be explained—just accepted with gratitude, as I strive to serve the Lord each new day.

❄ A STRANGE PLACE TO HOPE
Corrie Ten Boom

Rank upon rank we stood that hot September morning in 1944, more than a thousand women lining the railroad siding, one unspoken thought among us: *Not Germany!*

Beside me my sister Betsie swayed. I was fifty-two, Betsie fifty-nine. These eight months in a concentration camp since we had been caught concealing Jews in our home had been harder on her. But prisoners though we were, at least till now we had remained in Holland. And now when liberation must come any day, where were they taking us?

Behind us guards were shouting, prodding us with their guns. Instinctively my hand went to the string around my neck. From it, hanging down my back between my shoulder blades, was the small cloth bag that held our Bible, that forbidden book which had not only sustained Betsie and me throughout these months, but given us strength to share with our fellow prisoners. So far we had kept it hidden. But if we should go to Germany . . . We had heard tales of the prison inspections there.

A long line of empty boxcars was rolling slowly past. Now it clanged to a halt and a gaping freight door loomed in front of us. I helped Betsie over the steep side. The dark boxcar grew quickly crowded. We were pressed against the wall. It was a small European freight car, thirty or forty people jammed it. And still the guards drove women in, pushing, jabbing with their guns. It was only when eighty women were packed inside that the heavy door slid shut and we heard the iron bolts driven into place outside.

Women were sobbing and many fainted, although in the tight-wedged crowd they remained upright. The sun beat down on the motionless train, the temperature in the packed car rose. It was hours before the train gave a sudden lurch and began to move. Almost at once it stopped again, then again crawled forward. The rest of that day and all night long it was the same, stopping, starting, slamming, jerking. Once through a slit in the side of the car I saw trainmen carrying a length of twisted rail. Maybe the tracks ahead were destroyed. Maybe we would still be in Holland when liberation came.

But at dawn we rolled through the Dutch border town of Emmerich. We were in Germany.

For two more incredible days and two more nights we were carried deeper and deeper into the land of our fears. Worse than the crush of bodies and the filth was the thirst. Two or three times when the train was stopped the door was slid open a few inches and a pail of water passed in. But we had become animals, incapable of planning. Those near the door got it all.

At last, on the morning of the fourth day, the door was hauled open its full width. Only a few very young soldiers were there to order us out and march us off. No more were needed. We could scarcely walk, let alone resist. From the crest of a small hill we saw it, the end of our journey, a vast gray barracks city surrounded by double concrete walls.

"Ravensbrück!"

Like a whispered curse, the word passed back through the line. This was the notorious women's death camp itself, the very symbol to Dutch hearts of all that was evil. As we stumbled down the hill, I felt the Bible bumping on my back. As long as we had that, I thought, we could face even hell itself. But how could we conceal it through the inspection I knew lay ahead?

It was the middle of the night when Betsie and I reached the processing barracks. And there under the harsh ceiling lights we saw a dismaying sight. As each woman reached the head of the line she had to strip off every scrap of clothes, throw them all onto a pile guarded by soldiers, and walk naked past the scrutiny of a dozen guards into the shower room. Coming out of the shower room, she wore only the thin regulation prison dress and a pair of shoes.

Our Bible! How could we take it past so many watchful eyes?

"Oh, Betsie!" I began—and then stopped at the sight of her pain-whitened face. As a guard strode by I begged him in German to show us the toilets. He jerked his head in the direction of the shower room. "Use the drain holes!" he snapped.

Timidly Betsie and I stepped out of line and walked forward to the huge room with its row on row of overhead spigots. It was empty, waiting for the next batch of fifty naked and shivering women.

A few minutes later we would return here stripped of everything we possessed. And then we saw them, stacked in a corner, a pile of old wooden benches crawling with cockroaches, but to us the furniture of heaven itself.

In an instant I had slipped the little bag over my head and stuffed it behind the benches.

And so it was that when we were herded into that room ten minutes later, we were not poor, but rich. Rich in the care of Him who was God even of Ravensbrück.

Of course when I put on the flimsy prison dress, the Bible bulged beneath it. But that was His business, not mine. At the exit, guards were feeling every prisoner, front, back and sides. The woman ahead of me was searched. Behind me, Betsie was searched. They did not touch or even look at me.

Outside the building was a second ordeal, another line of guards examining each prisoner again. I slowed down as I reached them, but the captain shoved me roughly by the shoulder. "Move along! You're holding up the line!"

So Betsie and I came to our barracks at Ravensbrück. Before long we were holding clandestine Bible study groups for an ever-growing group of believers, and Barracks 28 became known throughout the camp as "the crazy place, where they hope."

Yes, hoped, in spite of all that human madness could do. We had learned that a stronger power had the final word, even here.

 ## SNOWFLAKES IN SEPTEMBER
Robert Hawkins

In September last year Sister Grace began forming a picture of a Christmas tree in her mind. As the director of pastoral care at Charleston's St. Francis Xavier Hospital, Sister Grace had been asked to decorate the tree that would be placed in the lobby of the Omni Hotel. The tree would have angels on it and snowflakes—lots of snowflakes, exquisite ones crocheted by hand. By Thanksgiving Sister Grace had acquired the angels, but the snowflakes were not to be found.

On the day before Thanksgiving, Doris Hartvig was admitted to the hospital for tests. Doris detested idleness, and she was soon busy at work with needles and yarn.

"Could you do a snowflake?" one of the nuns, Sister Mary Joseph, asked her.

"I can," Doris replied. In fact, not long ago she had bought a book that described how to crochet snowflakes. They weren't easy to do, and each one required a lot of time.

With renewed hope, Sister Grace went to see Doris. She described in detail the Christmas tree she had her heart set on: a blue bow on top, angels clinging to the branches, and lacy snowflakes hanging from the boughs.

"How many snowflakes do you need?" Doris finally asked. "We should have sixty," Sister Grace replied, "but there's no time to make that many."

Doris smiled. She reached under her bed and took out a bag of needlework, and then drew out one beautiful crocheted snowflake after another—forty, fifty, over sixty of them! They were ironed, starched, and ready to be hung.

In September Doris Hartvig had felt a great urge to crochet snowflakes. Now she knew why.

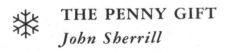

THE PENNY GIFT
John Sherrill

In 1987 while my wife and I were on a sixteen-month, free-lance writing stint in Europe, I had one more reminder that God does provide, even in unexpected ways. It was the year of the dollar devaluation. Week after week we watched the money we'd brought with us shrink against other currencies. As our cost of living soared, so did my anxiety.

I was at my most anxious one morning when I pulled into a self-service gas station just off one of the autobahns in Germany. The dollar's latest plunge had brought fuel to the equivalent of three dollars a gallon, and I was muttering to myself as I turned on the pump and watched the "amount due" dial spin faster than my eye could follow.

At that moment I noticed a young man ambling up the street in my direction. Wearing stained corduroy trousers and a torn sweater, he had the childlike look that so often goes with mental retardation. He stopped and stood watching me fill the tank.

As I withdrew the nozzle the young man edged closer and at first I thought he wanted a ride. But he had drawn a small purse from his pocket and was fumbling with the clasp. He emptied a few coins into his hand and with clumsy fingers selected one of them.

"Für dich," he said. *For you.* He held out a one-pfennig piece, worth less than half a U.S. cent.

"For me? But I don't need . . ."

I stopped short. In fact I had just been feeling very much in need. I stood there with the gasoline hose in one hand, the little copper in the other, watching God's spokesman wander off up the street.

 ## BECAUSE
—*Inez Franck*

> Because somebody cared today
> I knew God's love was strong;
> I found new hope to bear my cross
> And courage for my song.
> My neighbor's heart conveyed the love
> I needed for my pain;
> And happily I felt the faith
> To dream and smile again.

 ## THERE WAS PLENTY!
Adele Hooker

I've always had a strong faith in God, but I had never looked for miracles in my life. Until a few years ago . . .

When our family of four lived in Muskogee, Oklahoma, our income was so small we could barely pay for necessities. Sometimes it was cornflakes and milk for a week. On one such occasion, friends traveling through town stopped in, and to my amazement, my husband invited them for dinner.

I fidgeted, then went into my bedroom, knelt down, and asked God how I was to cook a dinner with no food in the house.

"But you have," came the answer that formed in my head. "You have meat in the freezer." (I didn't believe it.) "You have vegetables." (Maybe a can of beans.) "Make a stew. And you have flour. Make biscuits." (That I could do. I'm a good biscuit builder.)

I went to the kitchen to prove my inner voice wrong, but there in the freezer lay a small amount of hamburger, in the crisper lay half an onion and a carrot, and in the bin under the sink were two small potatoes.

I made the stew. Hadn't I asked God for help? What could I do but follow the directions that seemed to come to me? I put the flimsy fare in a pot, mixed up the biscuits, then set the table.

When I took up the stew there was barely enough to fill a medium-size serving bowl; I thought my husband and I would eat only biscuits and milk. But when I passed the stew around, behold, there was plenty. I served us and passed the bowl around again!

When our dinner was over, the guests thanked me for the delicious meal. And I gathered up leftovers.

We had *leftovers*. We did, we really did!

GOD

Preserves

OUR LIFE

Jehovah himself is caring for you! He . . . preserves your life.

—PSALM 121:1, 7, TLB

COURAGE
—*Paul Gerhardt, translated by John Wesley*

Give to the winds thy fears;
    Hope and be undismayed;
God hears thy sighs and counts thy tears,
    God shall lift up thy head.

Through waves and clouds and storms
    He gently clears thy way;
Wait thou His time; so shall this night
    Soon end in joyous day.

Leave to His sovereign sway
    To choose and to command;
So shalt thou wondering own, His way
    How wise, how strong His hand!

Far, far above thy thought
    His counsel shall appear,
When fully He the work hath wrought
    That caused thy needless fear.

Let us in life, in death,
    Thy steadfast truth declare,
And publish with our latest breath,
    Thy love and guardian care.

 ## THE MISSING SHOES
Elizabeth Sherrill

Of all times to have the airline lose my luggage! It was only my toiletries case with my one pair of good shoes, but of all places to wind up without them!

I'd flown out to Farmington, New Mexico, for a one-day

seminar sponsored by the Southwest Christian Writers' Association. "No one will care about your shoes," Margaret, the group's president, assured me.

Doubtless Margaret was right, but *of all times*. Even as I said it, a phrase came to mind: ". . . we should at all times, and in all places, give thanks unto Thee." At *all* times.

We met at the First Presbyterian Church. At the seminar's close, several writers came up to the speaker's stand. Suddenly there was a terrifying *crack*. Then a woman shouted, "Lie down! Everyone!"

Two men were outside, one of them brandishing a gun. The sound of exploding glass had come from the window. Later we learned that the men had been drinking and shooting at telephone poles. From the wall beyond the speaker's stand the police recovered the tip of an electric screwdriver fired from a homemade pistol.

While Margaret filled out the police report, the rest of us said good-bye, each no doubt recalling a step forward or a delay that had kept him or her out of the line of fire.

For my part, I was tracing a trajectory, from the window to the wall, an inch over the spot where I'd been standing. I was thinking of a pair of two-and-a-half-inch heels in a missing bag, and echoing a prayer: ". . . we should at all times, and in all places, give thanks to Thee, O Lord."

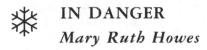

IN DANGER
Mary Ruth Howes

When I was growing up, I always liked to hear my father tell the story of a strange premonition he'd had as a young missionary in China. Dad's superior, a Mr. Sinton, had just left Luchow for an extended journey to outlying missions, when Dad was overwhelmed with the feeling that Mr. Sinton was in mortal danger. Every night, Dad prayed for his safety.

When Mr. Sinton returned, he told about having retired one night in a guest house where a tiny charcoal brazier burned. Later that evening Mr. Sinton had heard a loud mysterious pounding. Getting up, he went to the window, pushed it open, and looked out. No one was there. He started toward the door, but the next thing he knew, he was waking up flat on the floor. He had been overcome by toxic fumes from the brazier. Opening the window had saved his life!

Several years ago, when Dad was eighty-two, he called me at the office. "I had such a vivid dream early this morning," he said, "that I had to call you. I dreamed you were in danger. Is your house okay?"

I didn't want to do it, but remembering Dad and Mr. Sinton, I actually went home—only to discover my sick cat sleeping in front of the electric heater. No fire. No danger. I turned off the heater and, feeling foolish, returned to the office.

At home that night, I turned on the heater again, and fifteen minutes later the lights in the kitchen sizzled and flickered out. The motor on the heater had burned out, blowing the fuses and filling the kitchen with acrid smoke . . .

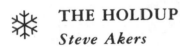

THE HOLDUP
Steve Akers

It was 9:00 P.M., February 6, 1981—closing time at the self-service Husky Gas Station in Albuquerque, New Mexico, where I'd been employed for about two months. As I counted out the day's receipts and put the money into a bank bag, I thought again how lucky I'd been to get this job. In the two years since I'd graduated from high school, I'd had a hard time finding good, steady work.

My mother, however, had not been pleased when I'd told her about my new job.

"Steve, I'm scared," she'd admitted. "I read all the time about robberies at those self-service stations. What if you get hurt?"

"Don't worry, Mom, I'll be fine," I'd reassured her. "Nothing is going to happen."

Now, looking forward to the dinner waiting for me at home, I slipped my fleece-lined denim jacket over my white T-shirt and blue corduroy pants, tucked the bag under one arm, and left the cashier's booth near the pumps to cross the parking lot to the storage shed where the safe was located. En route, I passed a man wearing a black windbreaker and black pants. He mumbled something to me, but I just nodded and went on. People on foot often cut across that parking lot, so I felt no alarm.

I stashed the money in the safe, then hurried outside and locked the shed. I'd started to turn back toward the booth when the same man I'd seen five minutes before stepped around from behind the shed and stopped me. A shock flashed through me at the sight of the black ski mask he'd pulled down over his face. The thing that turned my knees to Jell-O, though, was the gun he held in his black-gloved hand.

"Oh, my God," I gasped.

"That's right," he responded coolly.

Meaning, I knew, that he was about to hold me up, and he could see that I realized it. He motioned with the gun toward the booth, which was still unlocked and brightly lighted.

"Give me your money," he said.

He hadn't seen that bag under my arm, then. He didn't know I'd locked the money in the shed.

"I don't have any money," I told him.

He snorted in disbelief. "Don't give me that! Get in there and open that cash register!"

I moved toward the booth, trying to control my rubbery legs, which threatened to pitch me forward onto the asphalt.

"I'm telling you the truth," I insisted. "All I've got left are some rolls of change." And then, realizing I'd have to explain that, I did tell a lie: "The manager came by just a while ago and picked up the rest of the money. You're too late."

"Oh yeah? I'll have to see for myself."

He followed me into the booth. I glanced out toward the empty street, usually so busy. Surely someone would drive by and see what was happening, I told myself. All I had to do was try to stay calm until help arrived. Calm? My hands trembled as I groped for the lever on the register. The drawer slid open.

"Look, just change," I told him.

He began to curse. His eyes glared ferociously at me through the holes in the mask. He looked insane. Or high on dope. Still holding the gun on me, he began rummaging through the

shelves in the booth with his other hand, hunting for the bag of
money he seemed convinced was there.

"Pull the phone off the wall," he told me shortly.

The hole in the barrel of the gun, pointed at my chest, looked
as big to me as the hole in the end of a car's tailpipe. I grabbed
the phone with both hands and yanked. It didn't budge. I tried
again, but my arms had all the strength of wet spaghetti.
Finally, I picked up a small knife and cut through the cord.

He's just making sure I won't call the police, I said to myself. *Now
he'll leave, and I can go home.*

That's all I wanted right then—just to go home, to the safety
of my own four walls, to the love and support of my parents. I'd
tell my younger brother about the attempted robbery. He'd be
surprised, maybe not even believe me at first. Home . . .

The man peered through the window of the booth toward my
1973 Chevy Impala parked nearby.

"The money must be in your car," he snapped. "Get moving."

And he motioned again with the gun.

We left the booth and walked across the parking lot to the
car. He searched me there, looking for rolls of money in my
pockets. All he found was my wallet, which he kept. Then he
told me to open the car. Still keeping the gun pointed in my
direction, he felt around under the empty seats.

"Get in," he demanded. "You drive. Pretty soon I'll have you
drop me off somewhere."

I wanted to believe him. After all, I argued to myself, I had
nothing to give him. Sooner or later, he'd have to let me go.

We headed down the street in the car. When the man noticed
that the gas tank registered almost empty, he went into a rage.
He began to taunt me about making minimum wage at a gas
station and not being able to afford gas for my own car.

"Look at me, I can get plenty of money any time I want it,"
he boasted, "and I don't have to work for no crummy minimum
wage."

Then he told me that he was the man who had murdered Phil
Chacon, a popular Albuquerque policeman who had been shot
to death several months before. That murder was still unsolved.

My heart began to pound. My hands, damp with perspira-
tion, slipped on the surface of the steering wheel. For the first
time I looked at the fact that this man might kill me.

I needed help. I wanted to reach out to someone, anyone, but only God knew the danger I was in. Somehow my grandmother's face appeared in my mind, smiling at me the way she had when I was little. She'd been the one in our family with a strong belief in God. I'd wanted to believe in God, too—but for me, now as then, He seemed far away, out of reach. I just couldn't get in contact with Him, not the way she could.

Maybe it was because I'd always felt shy and insecure. Despite my parents' encouragement. Despite my grandmother's love. For I'd had some physical problems as a child that had kept me from developing as fast as my friends. While they shot up to become basketball and football stars, I remained slight of build. When they all began talking in deep voices and shaving every morning, I still looked, with my baby face, like a twelve-year-old. I gradually drew away from others at school, staying in my own corner, never speaking up in class. Even though I finally grew to be over six feet tall in my last two years of high school, my habit of staying in the background continued. That's another reason I'd never called on God—I thought someone as unimportant as I was didn't stand a chance of being heard.

Now, with this masked gunman sitting beside me, I *wanted* to be noticed. I kept hoping that someone would glance into our car at an intersection and see what was happening. One man in a car did pull up beside us, but then the light changed, and he took off, leaving me once more alone. Or was I alone?

Desperately, I began to pray: "God, if You're listening, I sure do need help. Maybe I am a nobody—maybe I've never done anything important—but I still don't want to die. Please—please, can You do something?"

The gunman told me what streets to take and where to turn. I saw at last that we were headed toward the airport near the south edge of town.

I said, "Look, I'll just let you out, and I'll go away, and you'll never hear from me again. You've only taken about fifteen dollars in change. I'll make that up out of my own pocket, and no one will ever know . . ."

The old coward bit. I'd fantasized, when I was younger, about all the brave things I'd do if I were ever in a jam. But actually looking into the barrel of a gun had sent my once-imagined courage right down the tubes.

"I haven't decided yet what to do with you. Just keep driving," he told me flatly.

When we came to a fork where the road circled to the left, into a loading area in front of the airport terminal building, the man had me veer instead to the right, down a winding dirt road that led out into the deserted dunes beyond the west end of the runways. In the glow of the headlights, I saw clumps of dead *chimisa* and trash-draped tumbleweeds. The rocky dunes rolled away on either side, bleak as the surface of the moon.

My chest felt constricted. My breathing had become fast and shallow.

"Lord, this really looks bad," I prayed silently. "Are You here? Are You with me?"

At the same time, a part of me kept rationalizing—maybe the man really didn't intend to kill me. Why should he, what would he gain? Maybe he'd just let me out and then steal my car. It would take me a while to get back to the main road where I could flag down a ride. But at least I'd be safe—the nightmare would be over, and I could go home . . .

"Stop," the man suddenly barked.

I pulled over toward the side of the road and turned off the key.

"Now get out. Leave the key in the ignition," he instructed.

I felt greatly relieved. *Good,* I thought, *he'll soon be gone.*

I climbed out and moved a few steps away, into the sand and tumbleweeds. The man slid over and got out too, coming to stand directly in front of me. Without saying another word, he brought the gun up, pointing it at my face.

It's amazing the number of thoughts that can flash through a person's mind in just one split second. I knew that I was going to die right then, and there was nothing I could do. I felt no sorrow for myself, but I grieved for my parents and what they would have to go through, trying to deal with such a terrible memory for the rest of their lives.

Well, Lord, this is it, I thought, becoming strangely calm.

All that, in the brief time it took the man to level the gun and pull the trigger.

I saw the flash, I heard the explosion. I waited to fall. Nothing happened. I stood on my feet, staring straight into the barrel. Had he missed? He couldn't have missed . . .

He pulled the trigger again. Again, I saw the flash and heard the explosion. Again, incredibly, I found myself still on my feet, facing that gun.

It misfired, I thought . . . but in that case, there would just have been a click, no flash or loud noise. Blanks? Even with those, there should have been a blast of some kind, powder burns, at that close range . . .

Where had those bullets gone?

I stared at the man, he stared at me. Then he looked in a puzzled way at the gun. He started to pull the trigger again, but seemed to change his mind. Instead, he taunted me about how close I'd come to death.

"You're lucky this time," he concluded, motioning toward the road. "Start walking."

I took off at once, stumbling through the sand and gravel. I couldn't believe that I was still alive. My mind reeled as I tried to take it in. To have the gun fail once seemed to me to be a miracle. But *twice* . . .

I snapped back to the present with a new shock of alarm, realizing that the car was rocketing up behind me like a race car roaring off the starting line. Before I could dive out of the way, the front bumper slammed into the backs of my legs. The car continued to speed forward as my body catapulted into the air and crashed headfirst onto the hood. With arms and legs flailing, I bounced over the windshield to the top of the car. From somewhere came the sound of breaking glass as my body careened about, somersaulting onto the trunk and then smacking face down into the road.

The car roared off. I lay there, stunned, with sand in my mouth. *But I was still alive!* Broken and helpless, no doubt, but alive . . .

Gingerly, carefully, I began to stir, testing for broken bones. I thought my legs would surely be fractured from the impact of the bumper, or my skull cracked and my neck snapped from the crash onto the hood. But all my joints worked with no trouble. I pushed to my knees, blinking against the sting of gravel in my left eye. Getting my feet under me, I rose to my full height under the brilliant glitter of the desert stars.

Broken bones? Not one! Only a few skinned places on my face and chest, a knot on my head, and the gravel in my eye. I'd been shot at twice and run down with my own car—and there I stood, virtually unhurt.

I heard myself saying aloud, "Thank You, thank You, thank You," over and over. And I knew that I was thanking God. Because to come out whole through three attempts on my life seems to me to be more than just coincidence. I really think the hand of God had to be at work in there somewhere.

I headed through the dunes toward the distant glow of lights in the fifteen-story hotel at the airport. With my clothes torn and dirty, with blood from the skinned places seeping through my T-shirt, I finally stumbled into the lobby and asked the startled desk clerk to phone for the police.

Later, the police and I found my car abandoned near the airport with two blue imprints from my pant legs ground into the bumper, a big dent in the hood where my head had hit, and a broken right window, which I must have kicked with one foot in my tumble over the car. Although the person who kidnapped me was never identified, there was a man of the same height and build convicted a few months later, along with another man, for the murder of policeman Phil Chacon. When I looked at the eyes of that man in a newspaper picture, I felt a shock jar my nerves. He might well have been the man in the ski mask, although I can't say for sure.

But one thing I do know for sure: my old sense of worthlessness is gone. It doesn't matter that I was never a big football star or a straight "A" student—when I called to God, He heard me. To Him, I was not unimportant. Now that my life has been spared, I'm determined to make the most of the talents I do have, whatever they may be.

Because of that resolve, I reported to work on time the day after I'd been kidnapped. The people in charge were impressed by that and soon promoted me, making me the youngest person in the city ever to become a Husky station manager.

I'm pleased by the promotion, of course. But even if that hadn't happened, I know God would still care for me anyway, no matter what I look like or what kind of so-called "crummy" salary I might be drawing.

I haven't yet been able to forgive the man who tried to kill me, but I'm working on it. Meanwhile—with God's help—I have a station to run.

❄ STRANGE DAY AT LAKE MUNKAMBA

William F. Pruitt

1968. Kasai Province, Zaire, Africa. As one of the missionaries who had been allowed to return to his former station in
what was once the Belgian Congo, I'd been "itinerating" for
several weeks—that is, visiting among the tribal missions in a
radius of about a hundred miles of my station in Moma. One
evening, after preaching and showing Cecil B. DeMille's 1927
classic film, *King of Kings,* I found that I was only about thirty
miles from our house on Lake Munkamba.

Almost on impulse I decided to spend the night there. It was
late, after eleven, and I was very tired. But I was also tired of
sleeping in my house-truck. Besides, I wanted to see the house
again.

This was no ordinary house. I don't mean architecturally,
though that too, given the local standards. It was extraordinary
because it was *ours*—the only home in Africa that was our very
own. We had built it years before as a hideaway for little family
vacations, and now, with Virginia and our two sons far away in
America, I longed even more to go there. The house represented
home and love and a security that often seemed elusive in those
days of internal African strife. I needed to be reminded of these
qualities once more.

As I drove toward the lake, I wondered in what condition I'd
find our hideaway this time. During the tribal fighting of the
early 1960s, it had been looted frequently. Doors and windows
and most of the furnishings—as well as the much-coveted tin
roof—had been carried away. Our roof now covered the local
chief's hut, but he had explained his taking it. "When I saw
those looters taking everything from your house," he had said,
"I knew you would want me instead of them to have that tin
roof!" Logic against which I could offer no rebuke.

At last I arrived. The house was still there. I fumbled my way
in the darkness through the bare living room to a cot in one of
the bedrooms and fell upon it. Exhausted, I was soon asleep.

I awakened early the next morning, looked about a little, and
said my prayers. I thanked God for another day of life and asked

Him to watch over me. Outside, through the morning mist, I saw a lone native fisherman on the shore nearby. There seemed to be no one else about. All was quiet. African quiet.

Time to get going, I told myself, and took my five-gallon jerry can to the spring and filled it with drinking water. Back at the house, I picked up my hat, and was about to leave when I caught sight of the fisherman again. It made me wish I had time to join him for a quick catch. *Well, someday,* I thought. *I'd just better check to see if that outboard motor I left last summer is still here.* With so much looting, there was no telling what might have become of a prize like an outboard motor.

I put down the jerry can and went to a small storeroom in the back of the house. It was windowless and gloomy inside, but I could see that the motor was still there. *That's a relief,* I thought, reaching down and patting it as if to say, "Good boy! Stay there, because you and I have some fishing to catch up on as soon as I can get a day off!"

At just that moment I became aware of something else in a corner of the room. It was black and coiled into a circle, as though very carefully placed there. *I don't remember having a rope like that,* I said to myself. I went over to have a closer look. I went *too* close.

Oh! Oh, dear Lord!

Zoom!

I felt a spray of liquid; it was as though a red-hot nail had been driven through my right eye!

Instantly I knew that what I had taken for a coiled rope was a spitting cobra, one of the most poisonous snakes in the world!

I screamed out loud and started running, running away, but I no sooner got to the door than I stumbled over the jerry can of water. Quickly I threw myself down on all fours and frantically splashed cold water into my face, trying to put out the fire that was spreading through my head.

A figure loomed over me. *"Muambi!** What is the matter?" It was the fisherman from the lake.

He looked at me, looked at the room, and ran away. *He knows what has happened,* I told myself. *He knows there's nothing he can do. He's probably gone to tell the chief that I am here and dying.* Every native African knows that the spitting cobra first blinds and

---

*"Preacher" or "Missionary" in the Tshiluba language.

paralyzes its victim with a deadly venom before attacking again.

The pain was excruciating. Where was the snake now? I went on splashing water on my face even though I knew my flailing might cause it to strike again.

Was I beginning to feel a numbing sensation creeping over me? It seemed that way, but I wasn't sure.

Minutes went by, maybe five, maybe ten. Three people entered the room. Strangers. A man and two women, white.

The man rushed to me. "What's happened?" he asked, and I stuttered out the word, "Cobra."

He ran outside and came back with a large stick. "There it is!" he yelled, as he lifted the stick and again and again brought it down on the snake's head, killing the creature—a seven-foot-long female carrying seven eggs!

One of the women came to me, checked my pulse, and tried to look into my blinded eye. "I'm a nurse," she said. Then she looked up at the other two people helplessly. "I don't know what to do, but I feel I *must* do something!" Then, as almost an afterthought, she opened her handbag and started searching for something. "A sample of an eye medication came to me in the mail the other day. I don't know anything about it," she said, addressing me, "but it's all we have. Shall I try it on you?"

I understood what she was really saying: The poor man is going to die anyway—or go blind; why not take the gamble?

I nodded and she put a few drops of the unknown prescription in my eye.

"It's just possible that the water you threw on your face helped," the nurse said. Now we waited to give the medication time to do its work, if it was going to.

A half hour passed. Just as the pain seemed to be easing, we heard footsteps. Another white man appeared, a stranger to the others. I was mystified. Where were all these people coming from? In those days in that part of Africa, no unidentified white man traveled alone.

Who was he? A French doctor, he said, on his way to a diamond mine fifty miles away. He'd heard of the beautiful Lake Munkamba and he'd detoured several miles off his route, parked his car a half mile away, and walked down to the shore of the lake.

The nurse explained to him what had happened to me. "Do you know how to treat venom in the eye?" she asked.

"Yes," he answered. He told us of an effective new antibiotic. In fact, he had used it successfully on a man at the diamond mine just the month before. Unfortunately, he didn't have any with him.

"Do you know anything about this?" the nurse asked, handing him the medication she had put in my eye.

He looked at it carefully. "That's it! That's it! That's the very one I was telling you about!"

The French doctor stayed for a while. Then, after giving instructions for applying the drops every thirty minutes and telling me to stay in bed for the next twenty-four hours, he left us, as quickly and mysteriously as he had arrived. None of us had even learned his name!

Now, however, I learned who my other saviors were: a Scottish missionary and his wife who were vacationing nearby and a nurse visiting them from an English mission. The kindly Scotsman took me to his house and put me to bed.

The next morning my eyesight was fully restored, my energy had returned, and my eye was not even red! Today I see as well from one eye as from the other.

But for the rest of that long day, and throughout the longer dark hours of the night, I lay reliving everything that had happened. It was easy enough to keep my body quiet, as the doctor had directed, but stilling the flow of emotion was impossible.

I prayed, of course, thanking God for His unfailing mercy and grace. I thanked Him for all of those who had had a part in my recovery and what I earnestly believed would be the restoration of my sight. I whistled hymns through my teeth and was relieved to feel no facial paralysis.

In the assurance of God's presence, I also slept. But during waking hours I played a game of "what if." What if:

   . . . I hadn't gone for water before checking the storeroom?

   . . . the fisherman had been on another part of the lake?

   . . . the missionaries and their guest hadn't been visiting?

   . . . the guest hadn't been a nurse?

   . . . there had been no sample of a new antibiotic in her purse?

   . . . the doctor had not appeared?

And so on and so on. This "what if" game went endlessly on.

And yet, I knew it wasn't a game at all. I knew that all of us at Lake Munkamba that morning had been participants with God in yet another of His unfathomable deeds. Had I been the object of an extraordinary series of coincidences? No, absolutely not. For in God's world, there are no coincidences.

ON A ROCK
Ron Chambers

I was going snorkeling in the Palm Beach inlet with my fourteen-year-old son, Don, and our diving instructor, Jerry. We were to swim out past the jetty, then float into the channel with the tide. Yet I hesitated. The breakers were enormous.

I put on the foam rubber wet-vest and Jerry's weight belt to offset the vest's buoyancy. Actually, I knew that the weight should be adjusted for each diver, I just didn't think about that at the time.

We dove in, Jerry and Don paddling along in front, with me right behind. As we swam out, the distance between us grew. *Better swim harder,* I thought. But I was swimming as hard as I could. Halfway out I saw Jerry and Don clear the end of the jetty.

The next instant, a wave slammed me against the rocks. Then another and another. The barnacles on the boulders slashed my arms and legs. The heavy weight around my waist was dragging me down. I tried to grab on to the rocks, but they were too large, too slippery, too sheer.

Exhausted, battered, I knew right then that I was going to die. I was pleasantly surprised that I felt prepared for it. I imagined myself standing in the presence of God, and the thought gave me great peace. I looked up and said quietly, "I'm ready, Father . . ."

Needless to say, I did not die. I'm still mystified by the way I was saved. To this day I'm drawn often to Psalm 27:5: "For in the time of trouble, he shall hide me in his pavilion: . . . he shall set me up upon a rock."

In my time of trouble, a huge wave suddenly crashed into the jetty and a swirling column of water lifted me up, up, up, six feet in the air, spun me around in a sitting position, and placed me safely on top of a rock.

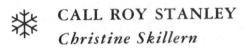

CALL ROY STANLEY
Christine Skillern

It was almost dark when I went into the kitchen to fix some supper. I didn't feel a bit hungry, but there are two rules we insulin-dependent diabetics must adhere to: take insulin regularly and don't skip meals.

So I shook some oatmeal into a pan of water, and set it to cooking on a front burner of my electric stove. I started across the kitchen to get milk from the refrigerator, but I never made it. My feet slipped out from under me and I fell hard, flat on my back, on the floor.

Oh, you've done it now, old girl.

I pushed and stretched and made every effort to get up, but I couldn't even sit up. Nothing I could do was going to get this overweight seventy-year-old body off the floor. I needed help. I thought about screaming, but who would hear me? I was a widow who lived alone and had already closed and locked all the windows and doors.

The telephone! I could call my sister, Martha. The telephone hung high on the wall, over near my bedroom door. Next to it was my broom, propped against the wall.

I dug my elbows into the rough texture of the floor covering and managed to slide on my back a couple of inches. Six or seven more shoves and a lot of panting put me near the phone. Using the broom, I gave it a *whack* that sent the handset banging to the floor. But to my dismay, I couldn't make a call. The dial was up on the phone.

Fear was beginning to gnaw at me. The burner under my oatmeal was glowing brightly. What would happen if the water boiled out? Would the metal pan melt and ruin my stove? Would it set my house on fire?

But there was nothing I could do. I was locked in my house with no way to contact the outside world, and no light except the glow from the electric burner.

Finally I whispered, "Lord Jesus, I'm so alone and I'm afraid. Please come and be here with me. Quiet me, Jesus, and protect me, and please take care of my pan of oatmeal."

The air began to chill as the evening grew longer. I hugged my arms about me and wished for a blanket. I dragged myself into the bedroom and looked longingly at the heavy spread on my bed. I could never pull that down. But there were some clothes lying on the cedar chest. Again I dug my elbows into the rug, and I pulled down a sweater and skirt to cover myself.

As the night grew blacker, I thought of the insulin shot I normally took after supper. What condition would I be in by morning? Was I going to die? My back was beginning to ache. I had no idea what damage I had done to myself. Panic began to smother me.

"Lord," I prayed, "don't leave me. Please stay with me and comfort me." Then I began to recite Scripture verses, mostly those I'd learned in Sunday school, one verse after another, until I slipped into a fitful sleep.

When the light of morning roused me, I thanked God that the long night was over and my house was not burned.

I said my morning prayers and made another attempt to get up from the floor. I could not move. My throat was dry and I was hungry. And how long could I go without insulin?

Surely a neighbor would telephone. Oh, no! The phone was off the hook. But then, maybe someone would come and knock on the door.

All morning I listened carefully but no knock came. I kept praying, "Jesus, please help me."

Around noon a thought flashed through my mind: *Call someone.*

Another thought: *Call your friends.*

"But the phone . . ." I said aloud.

I began to call out names. I started with my sister; I knew she'd be at work. Then I called my neighbors, one by one, pausing after each, listening for a knock.

I had run out of names to call when another sudden thought invaded my tired mind: *Call Roy Stanley.* Roy had stopped by two days earlier to pray with me, but he lived so far away.

Still the thought persisted: *Call Roy.*

So I began calling, "Roy, please come to me. I need you." I said it aloud, over and over without stopping.

It was about two o'clock when I heard a loud knocking on the back door. I yelled, "Come and help me. I need you."

Then I heard a series of heavy blows and a splintering of wood. Footsteps . . . and Roy was standing over me.

"Christine!" he exclaimed. "What are you doing on the floor?"

I told him.

Roy went to the kitchen to get some water for my parched throat. He phoned my sister and called for an ambulance. Then as we waited he told me how he happened to be there.

Roy and his wife were at home when he felt a strong urge to check on me. He told his wife, "I have to go to Christine. Something has happened to her."

When he knocked on my door, he got no answer, but something seemed to urge him, *Don't leave. Go to the back and knock again.* So he went around to the back door, knocked harder, and finally heard me calling, "Come and help me. I need you."

As the ambulance arrived, I felt a strange sense of elation. Jesus *had* been with me through the night. He'd brought Roy to rescue me. He'd answered every single one of my prayers. Even the one about the oatmeal. For when I finally thought about that burner, I said to Roy, "Will you please check on a pan of oatmeal I put on to cook last night? It must be burned black by now."

A strange expression crossed Roy's face. "I turned that burner off when I got the water for you," he said. "Did you say you put it on *last night?* Christine, that oatmeal is not burned. In fact, it's just ready to eat now!"

GOD

Speaks

IN VISIONS

Of old thou didst speak in a vision . . .
                    —PSALM 89:19, RSV

SEEING BEYOND
—*Mildred N. Hoyer*

> See the blossom on the bare branch;
> See the harvest in the tiny seed;
> See the wholeness in the illness;
> See God's order in the confusion;
> See life in the midst of death—
> See the substance of things unseen.

 ## THE SHARED DREAM
John Sherrill

In that mysterious Chapter 2 of the Book of Daniel, God saves Daniel's life by revealing to him the content of King Nebuchadnezzar's dream. I'd long been awed by this story, for it spoke of a dimension of the Spirit that was strange to me.

Then one stormy night my wife, Elizabeth, and I sat in front of a fire with our friends Len LeSourd and his wife, Catherine Marshall. After an hour of prayer we took a break. Catherine made cocoa and our talk turned to the subject of dreams.

"I've had a recurring dream," said Catherine, leaning back in her easy chair. "Every now and then I see myself in a—"

"Field," I said, interrupting. The room fell silent. Wind blew a puff of smoke down the chimney.

"How did you know that?" Catherine asked softly.

What could I say? . . . Only that as she had begun to describe her dream, I suddenly felt I knew its contents. I went on, "You are standing in a flat field. There is a stream running through the short, cropped grass . . ."

I knew from Catherine's expression that I was accurate. "The peculiar thing about the scene," I concluded, "is that the creek banks don't slant the way banks usually do. They're straight up and down, yet they're not made by machinery."

And Catherine whispered that this was indeed the content of her dream.

All of us were quiet for a while. I think each of us must have had the same thought. Here we were, people of the twentieth century, experiencing a mystery from the days of Daniel.

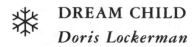

DREAM CHILD
Doris Lockerman

The woman's name was Mrs. Charles Smith. She was older than her years, and the long days of hard work on the farm had pulled at her face until there were no curves at all, only sweet, resigned lines. There was a peaceful look in her dark and strained eyes, the look of a woman who has not expected too much for a long time.

We were sitting in the farm house and she was telling me about her children.

She had borne three and lost all of them, she said, when they were babies. She never knew what it was that took them, maybe inadequate nourishment, perhaps the rigors of being born without a proper doctor. Whatever the cause, three of them had come here and been loved and then had died.

"Just as we felt they were doing pretty well."

Then one night, she said, she had a dream. She dreamed she would have another baby and she sobbed, "O Lord, don't send me another one, just to lose it!"

She said the voice in her dream told her not to fret, that this one would be a blessing . . .

Then Mrs. Smith looked across the bare room at a boy in his late teens, who sat looking out the window at some kittens and a puppy playing in the swept yard.

"You know, it was about that time that Ralph came to us." Her voice caressed him. "He can't hear," she said softly, "and he can't talk, but he's good. I don't know what we'd do without him."

Ralph turned then and smiled back at her, as if he had received a message. His eyes were blue and bright and intelligent. His work shirt was clean and stretched across strong, straight shoulders.

"He can read and write, and he works every day. He saves his money, and he bought us a little car. And we go to meetin' in it."

The boy flashed another smile and tried to speak. She whispered back at him, too low for ears to hear.

"He can read lips right well. My husband and I can talk to him without ever raising our voices. He understands us, and we understand him." She looked down, overcome by her own full heart.

"He came here from a cousin's home, when he was six, after his father died," she went on. "We raised him for our own. He was the child I dreamed about, the one who lived—he is the blessing."

THE DREAMED-ABOUT BABY
Katy Brown

The hot summer days of 1979 seemed to crawl by. My husband and I were waiting for our county adoption agency to complete the long process of clearing us so we could adopt a baby. We'd already gone through months of being interviewed and investigated—and we were told we would have another long wait even after we were approved.

Early one July morning, before dawn, I was startled awake by a vivid dream about a baby. What a happy dream *that* was— surely we'd have our baby soon!

But August passed without any developments, and September came before we even received our letter of clearance. Still, though our "credentials" were established, nothing happened. September dragged into October, and then November plodded by.

At last, two weeks before Christmas, the telephone call came. A woman at the adoption agency told me that the mother of a baby girl had reviewed the records of people and had chosen us. She gave me various details about the baby's birth and made an appointment for my husband and me to see her.

I hung up the phone and got out my desk calendar to mark

the date and time. Riffling through the pages, I saw a notation in my handwriting.

A prickle ran up my spine.

On the calendar page for July 20, I'd written "dreamed about baby."

That was the very day God had chosen for our adopted daughter to be born.

 ## JASON'S DREAM
Sharon Crisafulli

"Good night, Jason." I leaned down and gently kissed my eight-year-old son's forehead as he snuggled under his comforter. He was wearing his favorite baseball pajamas. His hair, always a little too long, fanned out over the pillow. His eyes were already closed when I turned to leave. But as I was pulling the door shut, he called to me.

"Mom? I just had a dream."

I returned to Jason's bedside. "Honey, you haven't even been to sleep yet. How could you have had a dream?"

"I don't know, Mom. It just came to me right after I said my prayers." His brown eyes held a serious expression. "I was in school, at my desk," he said in a strange matter-of-fact tone. "All of a sudden, I fell over onto the floor. People were staring at me. I was dead."

I sat with Jason until he fell asleep. His "dream" was disturbing. It seemed more than just a child's imagination.

Several times in my life I'd had similar experiences. I remember suddenly knowing my grandmother would die. Though she appeared to be perfectly healthy, she left us three days later. And I remember being certain a seemingly happy couple were having deep marital difficulties. I don't know how I knew; I just knew. Outwardly, they were the picture of marital bliss. A year later they admitted they had been near divorce at the time.

I went to bed wondering what Jason's dream was all about. Was it some kind of warning?

By the following week, however, the incident had been pushed to the back of my mind. Our home in Merritt Island,

Florida, was a busy place, and I had plenty of other things to
think about. Jason's school activities and caring for Nicole, his
lively three-year-old sister, for example. Then one night a week
later, I sat up abruptly in bed, wide awake. It was after
midnight, and Jack, my husband, was sleeping soundly. For a
moment I thought it was he who had woken me. But before I
could give it another thought, I was overwhelmed with the need
to pray—to pray for Jason.

As I eased out of bed, I felt tears streaming down my face. I
crept into his room and gathered him into my arms. I cradled
his warm body against mine as I prayed. I rocked him as I had
when he was a baby. Jason slept soundly through it all.

Then it was over. The need to pray ended as suddenly as it
had begun.

The next night it happened again—the sudden need to pray
for Jason. And again the night after that.

There was a time in my life when I would have felt silly
praying the way I did. There was a time when I would have told
no one. There was a time when I would have been afraid.

But now I knew it was time to pray, and so I prayed.

By the third morning, my midnight prayers were becoming
as predictable as the other routines of my life. As usual, I spent
the few minutes before the children woke sipping coffee and
savoring the quiet.

Nicole was usually the first to rise. But this morning she was
still snoozing even after Jason was up and dressed for school.

It was gloomy and overcast. As I looked out the window, I
was seized by a sense of sadness. Even as I made Jason's breakfast, my heart grew heavier by the moment.

I walked Jason to the end of our driveway. Right on time and
with a whoosh of air brakes, the school bus pulled to a stop
across the street, its red lights flashing.

Jason and I both looked up and down the busy highway. I
gave him a quick kiss and he was on his way.

He never made it to the bus. His left foot had barely touched
the pavement when a speeding station wagon came from nowhere and slammed into Jason, hurling his body fifteen feet
into the air. He came down hard, headfirst.

It all happened so fast. Now, there he was, lying in the
middle of the highway.

I fell to my knees beside him. His eyes were rolled back. His tongue was swollen and protruding. In a matter of seconds his right leg had swelled, straining the fabric of his jeans. His left arm was bent at a grotesque angle. I leaned close to his face and realized he wasn't breathing.

"No," I whispered. Then I lifted my head and screamed, "No, no, Lord, You can't let him die!"

A crowd gathered. They were all staring, horror-struck.

"Somebody call an ambulance!" I was amazed at the sudden control in my voice. "And get my husband. He's working in the orange grove down the road."

I bent over Jason and prayed aloud, "Dear God, I know You've raised people from the dead. Please raise up my son!"

I don't know how many people were in the crowd of on-lookers, yet in their midst I suddenly felt a distinct presence. I glanced up and found myself looking straight into the eyes of a bearded man standing a few feet away. He had reddish-brown hair and stood relaxed with both hands in his pockets. Though it was only a second or two, it seemed like an eternity before he spoke in a surprisingly soft voice: "I have oxygen in my car."

Moments later the man knelt beside me and gently placed the mask over Jason's face. Almost instantly Jason gasped and drew a long breath. Weeping with relief, I leaned over and whispered into his ear, "It's okay, son, just think about Jesus. You're going to be okay."

But when I turned to thank the mysterious stranger, he was gone. And although the road was jammed in both directions, no one saw him leave.

Jason was in the hospital for months. His thigh and arm were broken. He had a severe concussion. But amazingly, there was no permanent damage.

Now, ten years later, I still shudder when I think about what might have happened if I had not heeded those urges to pray, and pray hard. You see, I know that the bearded man who saved Jason's life wasn't just some passing motorist. He was part of something bigger. Something that involved Jason's dream. Something that required my waking three nights in a row to pray for Jason.

That mysterious man was part of a heaven-directed rescue, and he was there in answer to my prayers.

A GIANT BESIDE OUR HOUSE
Ron Gullion

I'm in our yard on Big Fir Court, gazing up at the mighty two-hundred-fifty-foot tree the street is named for. Rising from the corner of our property to the height of a twenty-story building, the great white fir dwarfs our home and everything in sight like some ancient giant. It gives the illusion of leaning ominously toward me, creaking and swaying ever so slightly in the rustling wind.

Look! It's not leaning, it's falling! It's toppling toward our house, gaining momentum, rushing to meet its shadow, until finally it crumples the roof and splinters through the living room and front bedroom with a sickening, thunderous roar. I let out a cry. Alison's room!

I awoke in a drenching sweat and sat straight up trying to blink away the terrifying vision. Another nightmare. I slipped out of bed and stole a peek into Alison's room. Our nine-year-old daughter was sleeping peacefully, as was eleven-year-old Heath across the hall. But I couldn't shake the irrational fear until I'd checked. This was not the first time I'd dreamed of such an accident. In another dream I'd seen a giant tree limb tearing loose and slamming down on Heath, leaving him crippled.

As a computer engineer, I deal with quantifiable information. I don't pay much attention to impractical things like dreams. But these nightmares were so vivid and frightening. I eased back into bed next to my wife, Nita, but not before looking out the window at the tree. There it stood, stately and still, its coarse bark ghostly pale in the faint moonlight.

A few nights later I had another dream, this one more puzzling than alarming:

I am in our yard and in front of me stands a white angel. The angel has a broken wing.

What did all these dreams mean?

Then one day I noticed a twenty-foot dead limb dangling from the fir. Out here in the Northwest we call a dangerous limb like that a widow maker. I remembered the dream about Heath. "Don't go near that tree," I warned him. That Saturday I enlisted a neighbor to help me rope it down; all week I'd worried about the precarious branch. Later I had some other dead limbs removed too.

Why am I so concerned about this tree? I wondered. *It's stood here for generations. It even survived the fierce Columbus Day storm of '62.*

My nightmares about the tree eventually subsided. Christmas season arrived and Nita and I rushed madly to get our shopping done. More than anything, Alison wanted a Cabbage Patch doll. We scoured the stores around Portland with no luck. Everywhere we went it was the same story. "Sorry, folks," said the clerk inevitably. "We sold out our Cabbage Patch dolls weeks ago."

Finally Nita settled on a handmade rag doll. It was thicker and heavier than the Cabbage Patch version, but there was something about it that caught our fancy. "Well," sighed Nita as we paid for it, "this will have to do."

"Alison will love it," I reassured her.

We arrived home to a surprise. Alison had impetuously decided to rearrange her room. She'd been talking about it for days, but Nita had implored her to wait until the holiday excitement died down. "Then I'll help you," she'd promised.

Instead Alison had recruited her brother for the task, getting Heath to help drag her heavy bed across the room. "I just wanted to get it done now, Mommy," she explained as Nita surveyed the scene with obvious displeasure. "It's important." Alison's toys and furniture spilled out into the hall. By bedtime, however, Alison had her room in order again and we could scarcely hide our admiration.

"See?" said Alison knowingly. "It's not such a big deal."

Outside I heard the wind whistle through the big fir.

A howling blizzard marked Christmas Eve. I drove home from work through swirling snow and pounding winds. I pulled into the driveway, turned up my collar, and hurried inside to get ready for church. Church was not one of my priorities even under the best circumstances, and on a night like this I didn't want to be anywhere but inside my house, Christmas Eve or not. But I'd promised.

At the service with Nita and the kids, I felt strangely detached as I hunched in the pew with my arms folded tightly, thinking about whether I even believed that God was a part of my life. I'd been raised in church but that was a long time ago.

Now I certainly didn't feel any "tidings of comfort and joy." God may have created the world and all its wonders, but I didn't see where that had much to do with my life. If God was real, He was much too remote for me to have faith in.

We arrived home late, and the wind and snow stung our faces as we walked up the driveway. Heath and Alison rushed inside to turn on the Christmas tree lights. From our bay window the blue lights cast a peaceful glow across the snowy yard. I draped my arm around Nita and led her in.

Wrapping paper flew as the children tore into their presents, and Nita and I settled back on the couch to view the happy chaos. Nita had turned the tree into a work of art. The crowning touch was a glorious blond angel perched high at the top. "It looks like Alison," I said.

Alison was so delighted with her big new doll that she granted it the honor of accompanying her to bed. "Told you she'd love it," I reminded Nita as we climbed under the covers. The moaning wind lulled us to sleep.

Roar! The explosive sound jolted the house. I hadn't been asleep long, and my startled, half-awake mind tried to separate fantasy from reality. *The dream again,* I thought. But then I sat bolt upright, and suddenly I knew. This was no dream. This time my nightmare was real. The tree really had fallen on our house!

I leapt out of bed and raced across the hall to Alison's room. "Daddy, help!" she was calling frantically. "I'm stuck!"

I couldn't budge the door. It was jammed shut. "Oh, my God," I whispered. "Don't move, honey!" I shouted through the door. "We'll get you out." I grabbed a flashlight and told Nita to call 911. "I'll see if I can get to her from outside."

I was horrified to find the tree filling the front hall, branches whipping in the gale. I stumbled through the family room to a side door. Outside I nearly collided with the massive trunk. Propped up on its giant ball of roots, which had been torn from the earth, it looked prehistoric. I crawled underneath as the rough bark tore at my robe and ripped my flesh. The wind sliced through me. Above the din I heard the distant wail of sirens.

Groping my way to Alison's window I aimed the flashlight beam inside and wiped the icy snow from my eyes. All I could see were branches, tattered insulation, and hunks of ceiling strewn about the trunk. Somewhere buried beneath the tree was my daughter, crying faintly, "Daddy! Daddy!"

Someone was standing beside me. "Alison! This is Captain McCullough of the fire department," he called. "Your daddy's with me. Can you move at all?"

"I think I can move my arm," came a brave little voice.

"Good. Push you hand up as high as you can."

Tiny fingers wriggled up through the debris. I breathed a tentative sigh of relief. Firemen rushed to set up lights and heat lamps. They fastened a plastic tarp over the rescue area. Captain McCullough turned to me and said quietly, "This isn't going to be easy, Mr. Gullion."

As I huddled with Nita, and neighbors looked after Heath, a terrifying game of pick-up sticks slowly unfolded. The night air was filled with the roar of chain saws and the reek of fir pitch as rescuers cut away at the tree and cautiously removed branches as they went. A slight shift of any debris could spell disaster.

Bit by bit they chipped away at the wreckage until, after an hour, Alison's head and shoulders emerged. Her right leg appeared to be crushed under the tree. A fallen two-by-six rafter clamped down on her torso. We could see Alison's new doll squeezed between her chest and the rafter. Apparently she'd fallen asleep clutching it.

McCullough shook his head grimly and called a halt to the work. "We can't risk it," he said. "Show me the crawl space." Moments later he played his flashlight on the area under Alison's room. Limbs a half foot in diameter pierced the floor and stabbed the ground beneath. Again McCullough shook his head. "We can't cut away the floor without disturbing the tree. *And that tree must not shift.*"

The subzero wind had intensified. Hours had passed and now there was the threat of Alison succumbing to hypothermia. Neighbors rushed in warm blankets and hot-water bottles. A paramedic put his wool ski cap on Alison's head. But I could see she was drifting, her big eyes fluttering. Once or twice her head rolled back. If we didn't get her leg out soon, the surgeons might have to amputate it to free her.

Only one chance was left: to lift the tree. A crane was out of the question. In this wind it would be too unstable. But

McCullough had called a towing company that used giant air bags to gently right overturned semitrailers. "It's a gamble," he warned me. "But we've run out of options."

Huge rubber bags were packed under the tree. A compressor roared to life. Slowly the bags filled with air and swelled against the giant fir. Despite the blizzard, I could see sweat bead up on McCullough's tensed brow. My hands trembled as Nita buried her head in my chest, afraid to look.

Suddenly I heard myself praying to the God whose very existence, just hours earlier, I'd doubted. You would have thought I'd be ashamed to ask His help now, but something told me I must. "Please, Lord," I begged, "spare her life. I believe You are there."

The shriek of the compressor was deafening. The bags bulged like great billows, but at first nothing gave.

Then there was movement! Inch by agonizing inch, the tree was lifted. A cry rose from the crowd as paramedics rushed to free Alison and whisk her to a waiting ambulance. Nita and I jumped in with her, and we roared off. Alison smiled weakly. "I'll be okay now, Daddy," she whispered, still grasping her new doll.

That overstuffed doll, it turned out, was possibly just enough of a cushion between the fallen two-by-six rafter and Alison's chest to have saved her life.

The doctors confirmed that she would recover. And Alison's leg was only broken, not crushed.

Christmas Day, Heath and I kicked through the rubble of our house. I'd been thinking about that desperate prayer I'd said, thinking about it a lot. In Alison's room I saw that the bulk of the fir had landed near the southeast wall—right where her bed had been before she'd impulsively moved it. On the trunk directly over where Alison lay when the tree came crashing through, I noticed a wide scar from a recently cut branch—one of those I'd felt such urgency to remove after my dream. That branch might have killed her.

Had God been trying to warn me all along about the tree? To protect us? Had I been blind to God's ways?

In the snow outside what used to be our living room I found the angel from our Christmas tree, the one that looked like Alison. Its wing was broken, just as the angel's wing in my dream had been. As I brushed it off and held it up, Heath came running. "Dad, Dad!" He grabbed the angel. "I've seen this before! In a dream! An angel with a broken wing just like this one!"

Dreams. Does God speak to us through them? The Bible says He does (Job 33:14–18), as well as in many other ways. This much I myself can say: Alison is safe and well. And God is, and always has been, watching over my family.

AFTER THE STORM
—*Hilen Letiro*

> The storms may come
> And limbs may break;
> Yet others bend
> Beneath the weight—
> Of heavy rain
> And windy breeze. . .
> A storm can mark
> The strongest trees.
>
> Life sometimes deals
> With us this way;
> In unseen trials
> We meet each day.
> It's not how much our bodies break
> Or how much they may bend;
> It's our outlook in our own life
> That helps our spirits mend.

THE REPEATED DREAM
Dorothy Nicholas

I've always been impressed by the way men and women in the Bible were guided by dreams—from the angels climbing Jacob's ladder to the dream warning Joseph to flee with his family to Egypt. I've always known such things were possible, but it was only in 1978 that I received such a dream myself.

A dear friend had a terminal illness and yearned to see her son again. The young man led a nomadic life. He didn't keep in touch very closely, and when he telephoned he rarely told her where he was.

Then one night I had a strange dream of huge stacks of *Esquire* magazines. I couldn't recall ever having read the magazine. I dismissed the dream as being of no significance, but it persisted. After I dreamed of a house built entirely out of *Esquire* magazines, my husband bought a copy. But I saw nothing helpful in it.

Then one day, a sudden thought hit me—the name of a hotel in Chicago that somehow I connected with the son. Did he live there? When I was visiting my friend, I contrived to sneak a peek at her address book. There, next to her son's name, among years of addresses, I saw the name of the hotel.

I wrote a letter to the son at that address, telling him of his mother's illness.

That was Monday. At eleven o'clock on Thursday night, my friend's son called collect from Chicago. He'd only been back at the hotel for a few days and he'd just received my letter. Shortly before his mother's death, he was reunited with her.

Dreams can be very real, and anytime I'm tempted to just brush one off, I remember the name of that hotel.

The Esquire, just like the magazine.

 ## THANK YOU, BILLIE
Grayce Shapiro

How much of a married couple's time together is spent in quiet pleasures, such as eating breakfast in the morning sun or enjoying an evening walk! Even late at night, when my husband was asleep, I enjoyed reading and writing and thinking, knowing he was there.

But when Billie died, those simple pleasures died with him. I was too tense to sleep. Each moment that I was awake and each tick of the clock reminded me that he wasn't there. I'd fall asleep only as dawn was breaking, and be wakened moments later by my alarm.

On one such morning I drowsily stumbled into the kitchen, put on the tea kettle, then wandered back into the bedroom and lay down on the bed. Instantly I was fast asleep, the deep exhausted sleep that finally comes, but never when I wanted it to. I had a dream. Billie and I were in the kitchen preparing coffee and toast. I saw him taking bread out of the bag and putting it in the toaster. I could hear him asking me if the water was boiling yet. Suddenly he became stern, saying, "Darling, you have the kettle on the wrong burner." And he repeated himself. Then he yelled, *"Darling, you have it on the wrong burner!"*

I jumped to my feet. There was an overpowering smell of gas in the room. The stove! The pilot light that I hadn't repaired! I dashed to the kitchen, turned off the stove, threw open the windows.

"Oh, thank You, God!" I cried out. And then I added the words that changed my life, "Thank you, Billie."

 ## THE CROWN OF THORNS
Caryll Houselander

As a child during World War I, I attended a French convent school. One of the nuns was from Bavaria. She spoke little English and very poor French, and she made no real contact with the children. Local police interrogated her as an "enemy alien," and there were even subtle murmurs in the community that she was a spy dressed as a nun. As the Germans advanced, so did the nun's loneliness and isolation.

One day as I passed the bootroom, the little cubicle where our shoes were kept, I saw the Bavarian nun sitting alone, cleaning shoes. I can see her now as if it were yesterday—a tall, gaunt woman with brilliant red cheeks, and eyes so dark that they looked black. There she was, wearing her large, cobalt-blue apron, with a child's pair of shoes on her lap.

Then I noticed the tears running down her rosy cheeks and falling onto the shoes. Abashed, I dropped my eyes to her large toil-worn hands. Hands, red and chapped, with blunted nails, which were folded in a way that expressed inconsolable grief.

We were both quite silent, I staring away not wanting to see her crying.

At last, when I raised my head, I saw an unbelievable sight: the nun's head was circled by a crown of thorns.

I shall not attempt to explain this. I am simply telling the thing as I saw it. That bowed head was weighed down under the crown.

I stood dumbfounded a few seconds, and then I told her, "I would not cry if I were wearing the crown of thorns like you are."

She looked startled, and asked, "What do you mean?"

I sat down beside her, and as I described to her what I had seen, a glow of joy enveloped her, dispelling the grief.

Together we polished the children's shoes.

 ## AT THE FOOT OF THE CROSS
Ernest Borgnine

Back in 1975 I was offered a part in the film *Jesus of Nazareth,* which through the years has been shown at Easter time on NBC television. Our cast, directed by the renowned Franco Zeffirelli, included Anne Bancroft as Mary Magdalene and Olivia Hussey as Mary, mother of Jesus. I played the part of the centurion who was present at the crucifixion, the one whose servant had been healed by Jesus.

Much of the film was shot in Tunisia on the Mediterranean during January and February of 1976. A cold, damp wind continually knocked over floodlights and stung us with desert sand. I was uncomfortable in my thick leather uniform. My neck ached under a ponderous metal helmet, and I even began to pity those ancient Roman soldiers who were called centurions because they commanded a hundred men.

When it came time for my scene during the crucifixion, the weather was chill and gray. The camera was to be focused on me at the foot of the cross, and so it was not necessary for Robert Powell, the actor who portrayed Jesus, to be there. Instead, Zeffirelli put a chalk mark on a piece of scenery beside the cameraman. "I want you to look up at that mark," he told me, "as if you were looking at Jesus."

"Okay," I said, moving into position and looking up at the mark as instructed.

"Ready?"

I hesitated. Somehow I wasn't ready. I was uneasy.

"Do you think it would be possible for somebody to read from the Bible the words Jesus said as He hung on the cross?" I asked.

I knew the words well from the days of my childhood in an Italian-American family in Connecticut, and I'd read them in preparation for the film. Even so, I wanted to hear them now.

"I will do it myself," Zeffirelli said. He found a Bible, opened it to the Book of Luke, and signaled for the camera to start rolling.

As Zeffirelli began reading Christ's words aloud, I stared up at that chalk mark, thinking what might have gone through the centurion's mind.

That poor Man up there, I thought. *I met Him when He healed my servant, who is like a son to me. Jesus says He is the Son of God, an unfortunate claim during these perilous times. But I know He is innocent of any crime.*

"Father, forgive them; for they know not what they do." The voice was Zeffirelli's, but the words burned into me—the words of Jesus (Luke 23:34–46).

Forgive me, *Father, for even being here,* was the centurion's prayer that formed in my thoughts. *I am so ashamed, so ashamed.*

"Verily I say unto thee, today shalt thou be with me in paradise," said Jesus to the thief hanging next to Him.

If Jesus can forgive that criminal, then He will forgive me, I thought. *I will lay down my sword and retire to my little farm outside of Rome.*

Then it happened.

As I stared upward, instead of the chalk mark, I suddenly saw the face of Jesus Christ, lifelike and clear. It was not the features of Robert Powell I was used to seeing, but the most beautiful, gentle visage I have ever known. Pain-seared, sweat-stained, with blood flowing down from thorns pressed deep, His face was still filled with compassion. He looked down at me through tragic, sorrowful eyes with an expression of love beyond description.

Then His cry rose against the desert wind. Not the voice of Zeffirelli, reading from the Bible, but the voice of Jesus Himself: "Father, into thy hands I commend my spirit."

In awe I watched Jesus' head slump to one side. I knew He was dead. A terrible grief welled within me, and completely oblivious of the camera, I started sobbing uncontrollably.

"Cut!" yelled Zeffirelli. Olivia Hussey and Anne Bancroft were crying too. I wiped my eyes and looked up again to where I had seen Jesus—He was gone.

Whether I saw a vision of Jesus that windswept day or whether it was only something in my mind, I do not know. It doesn't matter. For I do know that it was a profound spiritual experience and that I have not been quite the same person since. I believe that I take my faith more seriously. I like to think that I'm more forgiving than I used to be. As that centurion learned two thousand years ago, I too have found that you simply cannot come close to Jesus without being changed.

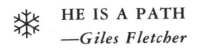 ## HE IS A PATH
—Giles Fletcher

> He is a path, if any be misled;
> He is a robe, if any naked be;
> If any chance to hunger, He is bread;
> If any be a bondman, He is free;
> If any be but weak, how strong is He!
> To dead men, life is He; to sick men, health;
> To blind men, sight; and to the needy, wealth . . .

GOD

Sends

HIS WORD

So they cried to the Lord in their trouble,
    and he saved them from their distress;
he sent his word to heal them
    and bring them alive out of the pit of death.
Let them thank the Lord for his enduring love
    and for the marvellous things he has done.
                    —PSALM 107:19–21, NEB

ST. PATRICK'S ARMOR
—From St. Patrick's breastplate

I bind unto myself today
The power of God to hold and lead,
His eye to watch, His might to stay,
His ear to hearken to my need,
The wisdom of my God to teach,
His hand to guide, His shield to ward;
The word of God to give me speech,
His heavenly host to be my guard.

THROUGH THE FIRE
Nellia B. Garber

The Bible was a gift from Bob, my husband, but it seemed to belong as much to our son, Doug, as it did to me. Doug and I read it together. We shared it in Bible study groups. Together we underlined God's promises. So when I received a new Bible, this familiar one became Doug's own.

Doug married, and eventually he and his family moved into a house not far from ours. Driving an eighteen-wheeler, he spent long hours away from home. He kept a little leather pocket Bible with him in the rig, but he made sure that "our" Bible stayed safely at home.

Then one bitter winter afternoon, there was a fire. He and Marla and the three boys were in despair. "The whole house burned down," Doug told us. "We lost everything."

For a week, neighbors, family, and friends tried to help them. They supplied clothes, money, food, furniture, and many prayers. Then one day Marla came over, smiling.

"Mom," she said, "look what I found in the rubble." Into my hands she laid an old Bible, soaking wet, its leather cover shriveled and brittle, but with all the pages intact. Doug's Bible—*our* Bible.

Immediately I began to dry it, first with a towel, then in the oven at 150 degrees. Slowly it became supple enough for me to turn its pages. When Doug came home, I said excitedly, "Open it up. Just let it fall open."

The Good Book opened and Doug read a passage we had underlined: *When thou passest through the waters, I will be with thee . . . when thou walkest through the fire, thou shalt not be burned; neither shall the flame kindle upon thee* (Isaiah 43:2).

God's promises. God's precious promises.

 # THE HIDDEN HAND OF GOD
Clared Holmes

One night a few years ago, for no apparent reason, I awakened in the middle of the night with a deep sense of foreboding. I checked the children but they were sleeping peacefully.

Before retiring I had, as usual, prayed for God's protection for the family and especially for my husband, Jim, who drove a cab on the night shift. Was God now trying to tell me something?

Once more I made the rounds of the house, sniffing the air for traces of leaking gas or the odor of burning; all was well.

I returned to my bedroom. The thought became clearer that Jim was in acute danger. I was overwhelmed with fear.

"God, please tell me what is Thy will. What am I to do?" I prayed, the sense of urgency keen. Opening my Bible at random, the words seemed to stand out: "Be still, and know that I am God" (Psalm 46:10).

Be still. Silence, fear. *Know that I am God.* Know without a doubt that God has His everlasting wings around every one of His children, guarding and protecting them.

Jim and I had always been very close spiritually, so now I spoke aloud to him across the miles:

"Jim, be still. *Be still.* Right where the danger is, there God is, protecting you. But you must *be still* and listen."

I glanced at the clock. It was 2:07 A.M. I felt God's presence very close and I knew all was well.

The next morning when Jim returned home, he related a

curious happening. He had been about to descend one of San Francisco's steepest hills with two passengers when he heard a voice say, "Be still." He lifted a foot from the throttle, half turned in his seat, and asked, "Did you speak?" The passengers claimed they had not spoken. He turned, was about to proceed, when he heard again, "Be still."

He was rolling slowly, but now the thought came to him: *Test your brakes.* Just as the front wheels went over the crest of the hill, he put his foot on the brake and discovered they were quite useless. He made an abrupt turn and rammed the cab against a cement retaining wall. The front of the cab was mangled, but no one was injured.

"If I'd gone two feet farther," Jim said, "we could have had a terrible disaster. I couldn't have stopped the car and we might have hit other autos at the intersection.

"It must have been God speaking to me, telling me to be still so I could hear the thought to test my brakes."

"What time was this?" I asked.

"I picked up the passengers a few minutes after two," he replied.

 # FAREWELL ON THE MOUNTAINSIDE
Betty Banner

Snow had fallen all night and the mountain was a fairyland of whiteness. I was twenty-one years old and expecting my first baby in the spring. All my life until the past ten months had been spent in a fairly good-sized town, and the deep, narrow valley between the tall mountain and ridge where I was living with my husband and his mother was a constant source of interest and new experiences. The mountain folks I had come to know and the many customs of the "old folks" that they still cherished had formed a new world for me.

During the previous summer I had insisted that we attend the little white Methodist church about two miles down the valley, and even though the circuit-rider preacher only came once a month, I had helped organize a Sunday school for the in-between time.

This particular morning was Monday and "washday" by an infallible rule of the mountain community. Snow or no snow, we washed, and I hummed a gay little tune as I helped my mother-in-law fill the zinc tubs on the glowing kitchen range and sorted the clothes for washing. My thoughts were of the coming baby, and the warm, steamy kitchen, accentuated by the white coldness seen through the windows, gave me a feeling of security and snugness. In thinking of my own happiness, I talked with my mother-in-law about the pity we felt for a young couple, who, we had been told, had lost their three-week-old baby during the night just the day before. We were still speculating as to what might have caused such a death when a knock at the back door gave us both a start.

Opening the door we were even more startled to see standing there the very same father of the dead child we had just been discussing. His name was John and he seemed hesitant to come into the kitchen but stood twirling his cap in his hands and staring at his feet. All of a sudden he took a deep breath and blurted out, "Betty, we was aimin' to bury our baby today, and now this snow an' all, and the preacher can't get acrost the ridge, and from the way hit's snowin' can't reckon when he could get here." Then as we started to sympathize, he said, "My Maude . . . she's right smart tore up, and ain't able to git outta bed this mornin', but she says we just can't put our baby away 'lessen we have a service over her, and you're the only one I knowed round here I thought could do it."

It was a moment before my stunned brain could take it in that he was talking to and about me. I couldn't believe he was asking me to do the service. I started to stammer that I couldn't possibly preach a funeral, and besides we couldn't get the car out of the shed even to go two miles down the valley. I might have saved my breath, for he stood there with such grief and stubborn determination in his eyes that I felt like I was butting my head against a brick wall for all the progress I was making.

Then he said quietly, "How'd you feel if it was your young 'un?" That did it. I had no answer for that, so I dumbly wiped my still wet hands on my apron and began to untie it. I don't remember another word spoken as I pulled on high rubber boots and coat and muffler. All I could do was pray frantically over and over, "Dear God, help me, give me words to help. Help me to say what will comfort them, Lord. . . . "

Leaving word about where I was going for my husband who was feeding cattle, I set out with John for the long cold walk to the church. Slipping, sliding, often wading drifts, with no conversation between us, the silent white flakes of snow pounding in our faces, we reached the church at last and went in. My heart came up into my throat. In spite of the snow, the little chapel was filled with mountain folks, and the little homemade coffin rested under a wreath of crepe-paper flowers in front of the rough altar.

Such a small, crude little chapel, with its oil lamps hanging on the walls, yet in that moment it seemed to me as vast and awesome as St. Patrick's Cathedral, which I once visited. I thought I'd never reach the front and as I stumbled down the aisle, my frantic brain could only repeat the same prayer: "Dear God, help me, help me. Let me say the words that will help them feel Your presence."

When I turned to face the silent congregation, I had to grip the pine pulpit tightly to keep from just going down. It hit me, too, that there was not even a Bible in front of me and I had not thought to bring mine!

As I realized that, I thought, *Well, this is it. I cannot go any further.* And then my eyes fell on that pitiful little box. Then and there God worked a miracle for me, just as surely as if He had reached out and touched my mind and lips. From somewhere unknown, the words came, disjointed as to correctness of quotation I am sure, but essentially those I had heard from early childhood on similar occasions. "I am the resurrection and the life . . ." "Casting all your care upon him for he careth for you." "Suffer the children to come unto me . . . for of such is the kingdom of heaven." On and on the words came, as if a scroll were being unwound before my eyes. Last of all came a prayer—and that was mine, for as I felt my own unborn child stir within me, my petition for a grieving mother in a log cabin on that lonely mountainside found the right words for the final commitment of "earth to earth" at the tiny graveside.

I am now a grandmother, and through the years I have faced many trials and crosses where I have felt like giving up before I started. But always the memory of "my miracle" comes to me and I go on, for surely the loving God who could give an ignorant twenty-one-year-old girl a funeral service can guide a more mature woman through any difficulty. Always, too, in such a crisis I seem to see John's face and hear the simple words he spoke as I turned from that grave toward home.

"Thank you—I knowed you could do it."

 ## SHOW ME YOU LOVE ME, LORD
Janet Martin

Do you believe in miracles? I do, because one happened to me. Let me tell you about it.

In those days, I was a virtual newlywed, having been married two years to a young dentist. Wyman and I were living in Altus, Oklahoma, then; he was serving a tour with Uncle Sam at the Air Force base in that Panhandle town.

The wind blows constantly in Altus, moaning down chimneys, whirling dust into blood-red sunsets, and piling mounds of loose, scraggly tumbleweed against front doors. It can be a lonely sound, wind, particularly when it heralds the approach of midwestern winter.

I was not lonely that first November away from my Georgia home, however. Busy with my first house, looking forward to a first Christmas in a new town, I was anticipating another first—the coming of a child into our lives.

Due in January, he (I simply knew it was a boy) would fill up the extra bedroom with diapers and stuffed animals, smells of talcum powder and sounds of contentment. His crib had been ordered; his room newly painted. It was about two weeks before Thanksgiving, and I looked like I had swallowed the turkey.

"It's going to be a football player," my husband laughed as I waddled, seven months pregnant, from stove to table, fixing dinner the night of November 7, 1971.

"Wait a minute!" I shot back. "I still look pretty good from the neck up. Focus on that!"

The night was cold. After dinner we lit a fire, watched the dancing flames, talked of quiet hopes, and called it a day.

Then, without warning, in the middle of the night, a gush of water, and I awoke, knowing something was terribly wrong. I called the doctor.

"Your water has probably broken," he said. "You might go into labor or the sac might seal off. Call me if it doesn't, but in the meantime, lie down. Keep me informed."

Later, I learned, Dr. Richard Hagood had turned from the receiver to his wife, Dana, a friend of mine. "Janet's carrying twins," he said worriedly.

Meanwhile, I hung up the telephone, strangely calm. I told Wyman what the doctor had said, then lay down on the bed and went to sleep.

The dawn of November 8 seeped around the window shade, which rattled loosely in the wind. I sensed its coming and knew I would be going to the hospital that day.

In the emergency room I smiled at my doctor friend as he strode in carrying X rays that had been taken moments before. "Janet," he said, "I've got something to show you."

Slap, slap went the X-ray film, gray against the fluorescent view box on the wall. There, glowing from the screen, were two tiny shapes, twins, impatient to be born two months early.

Because the hospital in Altus was small, Dr. Hagood thought it urgent that I be in a larger hospital facility, one especially equipped to handle "preemies." Wilford Hall Hospital, the medical center at Lackland Air Force Base, San Antonio, Texas, was such a place. That was where I should go, the doctors decided, and somehow they arranged for a plane to fly me there. My husband, close by my side, was pale, anxious. He knew the survival odds on premature infants. I did not.

At Wilford Hall, everyone in the labor room was kind, but businesslike. A nurse came in, heavy, motherly. "These are your first," she stated, rather than asking. I nodded. "I hope they're girls," she smiled. Then she said something I thought was strange: "Girls do better."

But they were boys. Blond, blue-eyed, curly haired, and beautiful. They lived only twenty-four hours.

Back in Oklahoma, numb with shock, I greeted my concerned friends with a blank face. I looked at my husband's face,

lined with grief, and felt remote from everything. The doorbell
rang. A delivery boy had brought the baby crib. Would I sign
for it?

Wyman and I boxed up the tiny pink and blue clothes we had
purchased for a layette. My mother, who had flown out to be
with us, suggested that we close the nursery door for a while.
We did. And I closed the door to my heart.

Time moved on. Holidays—Thanksgiving, Christmas—
came and went. I hardly noticed. Somehow Wyman and I
finished our Air Force tour, aided by the comfort and support of
good friends. Our departure date was set. We were going back
to Georgia. We were leaving the lonely prairie wind that had
blown my grief-stricken thoughts around and around until I
thought I would go mad.

Would my heart ever heal? Would the sadness ever soften?
Would the questions ever cease?

The morning we were to set off for Georgia, I sat down amid
the packed cardboard boxes and opened my Bible. Pressing two
thumbs together at random on the gilt-edged pages, I spread
the book out across my knees. Incredulously, I read words I had
never seen before: "Sing, O barren one, who did not bear; break
forth into singing and cry aloud. . . . For the children of the
desolate one will be more. . . ."

Isaiah, the prophet, continued to speak, especially to me, it
seemed, in this marvelous fifty-fourth chapter! "Enlarge the
place of your tent, and let the curtains of your habitations be
stretched out; hold not back. . . ." For a moment, reading
those ancient words, I felt a flicker of hope.

But the house in Georgia seemed big, too big for a young
couple with no children. While my husband was at work, I
walked the hollow halls. I closed barren bedroom doors. I
listened for voices that would never frolic here, and I came face-
to-face with despair.

Enlarge the place of your tent. But this tent only housed the
wind.

I kept trying, however. I sewed curtains, cleaned carpets. I
bought a cat and lavished attention on her as if she were human.
Wyman and I thought up things to do, places to go, friends to
see. But something was missing. We both knew it. And we
could not seem to do anything about it.

A year passed, a long terrible year. Another was well on its way, and despite our longings, our prayers, there was no baby on our horizon.

I went to work to forget. A journalism job — new challenges, the exciting smell of newspapers coming black and smudgy off giant rollers—these things helped. But busyness was only a temporary relief.

Finally in desperation I went to the Source. I opened the door of my heart to God. Alone one morning early in February, I stretched out my arms flat across the kitchen table, bent my head, and cried. I told the Author of life I could not bear the hurt and emptiness any more. I wanted to die.

"Lord," I sobbed brokenly, "if I must go on living, You have got to show me You love me. I can't help it, Lord. Maybe it's not right to ask for a sign, but I feel so alone, I feel You don't love me, Lord. Please, if it's not too much to ask, show me You do."

Slowly, quietly, spring came to Georgia. Swollen dogwood buds burst into tiny white crosses. Crocuses peered through the sodden red clay. The pine tree pollen blew in the gentle Southern breezes, sprinkling all nature with a powdery yellow glaze.

And as life stirred all around us, my prayer was heard. We were expecting a baby again.

Enlarge the place of your tent. Hold not back . . .

We bought a tiny yellow cotton nightgown. Months moved by, and we hung curtains in one of the empty bedrooms. Then, almost trembling, we unpacked the unused baby crib; we unboxed tiny pink and blue clothes.

When the seventh month of pregnancy came, I was afraid. I had terrible dreams. But the seventh month passed, and the eighth.

Then, early in the ninth month, it happened again. I was lying quietly on the bed that afternoon, reading a book. Suddenly, my water broke.

Frantically, I called the doctor. "Don't you see?" I screamed at him. "It is November eighth! The twins were born this way exactly two years ago today!"

"I understand that, Janet," Dr. Robert Davis replied calmly. "But I believe the Lord works in mysterious ways. I'll meet you at the hospital. Get going."

Show me You love me, Lord . . .

Our daughter was born safe and whole, within minutes of the time when the twins had come. Early the next morning, when the nurses rolled that tiny pink bundle into my room, I cried for joy. I took little Kristen in my arms, kissed her beet-red nose, and said "Thank You" to the God who had showed me that He loved me.

There are some, I know, who would look upon all this as coincidence. There might even be statistical wizards who could calculate the probability of a same birth date—even the same birth hour—within the realm of reasonable expectation. But their opinions would be irrelevant to me.

All I knew then, and what I still know, is that death was swallowed up in life.

And because of that, because the Lord took personal care to express His love to me in that special way, I believe in miracles. And today when I read the fifty-fourth chapter of Isaiah, I know why He issued such a strange command to that newly barren young woman in Oklahoma years ago. He was telling me that in the face of trouble I should have faith. I should sing.

 ## A CIRCLE OF LITTLE RED CHAIRS
Philip Turner

The May night was balmy, with no hint of disaster in the moonlit sky, when our neighbor, a pilot, said, "Let's take a midnight spin over the lake." Just as casually as that. My wife, Bobbie, and I told Bob we'd love to go. Just as casually as that, on Memorial Day weekend in 1975, our lives were changed . . .

At Shelbyville's small airport, deserted at that hour, I watched Bobbie climb into the little four-seater Beech Musketeer first, her tall athletic figure folding into the space behind the tiny cockpit. I took the copilot's seat while Bob ran the safety checks. This was a good little adventure for us. Bobbie and I hadn't been spending much time together in the last year or so. My law practice kept me running six days a week. As for Bobbie, with the kids both in school, she needed more to do than play golf, so she'd begun to travel all over Illinois as an instructor for Weight Watchers. We communicated with notes on the kitchen table. Bobbie and I were drifting apart, and both of us knew it.

In a few minutes we'd left the runway lights behind and were climbing into that crystal clear sky. Below us in the moonlight Shelbyville was asleep. I could see my parents' house where the children were sleeping over. The law office I shared with my father. The church where Bobbie and the kids went. They went, but I didn't. Sunday was the day I caught up on my sleep.

I wasn't an atheist, I'd explained to the kids. As a lawyer I acknowledged a Divine Law. But I didn't expect that Law to take time out from running the universe to look after me. My own hard work did that. I'd already become state's attorney for Shelby County, and—

"Look there!" Bob said.

The cloud dropped out of nowhere, a "low scud" suddenly obscuring the moon. Bob nosed the plane downward to stay beneath it.

"Better go back," he decided. No telling how far the fog extended.

Bob began a slow 180-degree turn, descending all the while to keep below that rapidly falling ceiling. I could see the runway lights ahead of us now, off to the left.

It's the last thing I remember. The rest of what happened I pieced together weeks later from other people.

They say it was the nose wheel of the Musketeer that hit the power line, flipping the plane over. In the split second before it hit the ground upside down, Bob's reflexes were quick enough to switch off the electrical system, preventing us all from being cremated on the spot.

Bobbie was somehow thrown over my head and through the side window onto the ground.

I am told that I remained suspended head downward in my seat belt, with over a hundred bone fractures.

Trapped inside the smashed cockpit and badly injured himself, Bob could only wonder why rescue was so long in coming. From the tail of the plane, he knew, an automatic crash-signal would be broadcasting our whereabouts.

What Bob did not know was that the only electronically equipped facility in range, the Federal Aviation Agency's flight

service station in Decatur, twenty-five miles away, never received the signal. Our plane was upside down, the transmitter
stuck in the ground. In the normal course of events it would be
next morning at the soonest, long after the three of us were
dead, before anyone happened out in this direction and spotted
the wreckage of the Musketeer.

A few miles away, however, a woman who happened to be a
client of mine was watching a late TV show when all the lights
in her house went out. She called the electric company, who
roused a sleepy repairman. He found the line into the woman's
house intact and, climbing back into his truck, set out to look
for the break.

An hour and a half after the accident he spotted the downed
plane and radioed the sheriff. As chief law enforcement officer
for the county I had worked with the sheriff for several years; my
face was so swollen he never recognized me. I don't remember
the trip by ambulance to the local hospital, where our injuries
were treated. Nor being transferred together with Bobbie and
Bob to the larger hospital in Decatur.

I first regained consciousness in the intensive-care unit. Dim-
ly I became aware of the small curtained cubicle, the whir of
machinery. I seemed to recall being in an airplane, and that
Bobbie had been with me, but the scattered images refused to
come together.

What filled my mind was something else. Something glowing, alive—and impossibly huge. A presence unimaginably
vast was somehow with me in that tiny space. More than with
me. It was containing me, enfolding me, cradling me. I was
being *held* as a baby is held. A baby who has only just opened its
eyes to behold the Father who has carried it all along.

Hours passed. Doctors bent over, tubes were removed and
inserted, and all the while I was wrapped in that bright cocoon I
could only call Love.

As my head grew clearer, and still that love embraced me, I
began to argue with it. I was accustomed, after all, to argue
cases on their merit. Why should God love me? God was the
only name I could give to the glory that radiated in that six-by-
three cubicle. But I hadn't given God much of a thought in
thirty years.

Not that we loved God, 1 John 4:10 corrected me, *but that he
loved us. . . .*

Who hath saved us, I recalled too, from 2 Timothy 1:9, *not according to our works, but according to his own purpose and grace.*

I blinked my eyes. Where were these verses coming from? I hadn't opened a Bible in years, and I certainly had never memorized—

And then I remembered Sunday school (I must have been five years old), a little circle of small red chairs, a cluster of children, and old Mrs. Wolf with a Bible open on her lap. She drilled us on Bible verses. Those who could recite the memory verses got a pretty card to keep. I didn't collect many cards; I was one of Mrs. Wolf's disappointments.

The painful days in the ICU dragged on. Strange, above the rattle of instrument carts, I heard Mrs. Wolf's voice:

Fear not. . . .

God so loved the world. . . .

Is there any thing too hard for me? . . .

I needed these words of hope and promise, for by now I knew that in the crash Bobbie's spine had been crushed. If she lived she would be a quadriplegic, not expected to regain the use of muscles below her neck.

As soon as my own broken bones were in casts I was helped down the corridor to Bobbie's room, where she lay strapped to a Stryker frame that rotated her body every hour. She was in too much pain for me to tell her in detail about the spiritual changes in my life. I could only stand in the doorway saying over and over, "God loves you, Bobbie. And I love you."

The kids had been staying at their grandparents' since the crash and that's where I went too, after my discharge. I was supposed to stay in bed, but that first Sunday out of the hospital I asked my aunt to drive me to church. I couldn't wait to learn more about the Immensity that had met me in a six-by-three cubicle. The Law that governed galaxies had turned out to be a very personal Love as well.

When she could be moved, Bobbie was taken to Chicago, where bone from her leg was used to fuse a crushed neck vertebra. The touch-and-go surgery was successful in restoring movement to her arms. A month later she entered a rehabilitation center to learn the skills of living in a wheelchair.

A year after the accident Bobbie came back to a changed home. The special doors and access ramps were only the external alterations. Far more profound were the changes inside ourselves. Having come so close to death, every day of life is for both of us an inexpressible miracle. Time with Bobbie—to talk, to laugh, to hold hands—is far too important for me to crowd my schedule with mere business.

I had time with my children too in the years before they went off to college. In the months while Bobbie struggled for life and strength, I prayed with them for the first time. And when they said, "Do we have to go to church today?" I was the one who said, "Yes."

It wasn't in law school, I told them, that I learned the things that mattered, but in a circle of little red chairs.